Historical Recipes from

THE PURE FOOD CLUB of JACKSON HOLE

& More

by JUDY S. CLAYTON
with JEAN STEWART

Cover Photo: Jackson's all-woman government
L-R, Mae Deloney; Rose Crabtree; Grace Miller,
mayor; Faustina Haight; and Genevieve Van Vleck

Collection of the Jackson Hole Historical Society & Museum

This cookbook is a product of
Cookbooks by Morris Press *Type 'N $ave™* program.
All recipes were typed by the author.

Copyright © 2001
Judy S. Clayton & Cookbooks by Morris Press

All rights reserved. Reproduction in whole or in
part without written permission is prohibited.

Printed in the U.S.A. by Cookbooks by Morris Press
P.O. Box 2110 • Kearney, NE 68848

Dedication

This book is dedicated to my parents, to my dear and loving husband Wayne, and to our children who have supported and encouraged me in this and nearly every foolhardy adventure I've engaged in. It is also dedicated to the pioneers who settled this valley and preserved it for the rest of us. Jackson Hole is unique, not only because of its stunning beauty, but because of its people. To those old-timers who remain and remember, thank you for sharing your memories with us. You are the true treasure of Jackson Hole.

Acknowledgments

This book is the product of the efforts of hundreds of people who have shared their stories and their recipes with us at Teton Views. A special thanks to all of you.

Thanks to Jean Van Vleck Stewart, who first told me about the Pure Food Club of Jackson Hole and who has been so generous in sharing her mother's priceless hand-written cookbook and stories of those whose recipes are preserved in it. Her insights, recollections, encouragement, and enthusiasm have been boundless. Anna Ferrin's incisive memory and stories have been incredibly helpful. Reference librarians at the Teton County Library did a massive, intense, but largely fruitless search for national information about the Pure Food Club to help me meet my deadline. I will be forever grateful.

Part of the proceeds of the sale of these books will be donated to the Jackson Hole Historical Society and Museum, in appreciation of their tireless efforts in helping with research, photos, and inspiration, not only for this volume, but for our weekly publication, Teton Views. Their collection of artifacts and information is a prize too few appreciate and explore.

Thanks to Sharon and Jim Grutzmacher, who have printed every issue of Teton Views and given endless advice and encouragement. Thanks also to Laurie Genzer, Marge Ryan, Jackie Richardson, Jill Russell, and Jean Stewart, who proofread this volume.

Tent Dining in Grand Teton National Park
Collection of the Jackson Hole Historical Society & Museum

A Little About Early Jackson Hole Cooks and Cooking

Jackson Hole's abundance of wild game led the first visitors to the valley—Native Americans. However, in spite of wild meat, times were often lean. French trappers named one band, a group of Blackfeet, the Gros Ventre Indians. Several places in Jackson Hole were named for them. Gros Ventre means "big bellies." Some historians say they were so named because the Indians often signed that they were hungry by passing both hands in front of their stomachs. Others believe they were named because their stomachs were swollen, due to starvation.

Our history of Native Americans, mountain men, trappers, and early settlers with camp fires and Dutch ovens encouraged innovation with scant supplies for the creation of tasty, life-sustaining foods. Mountain men who came in search of furs relied heavily on wild meat. Trapper

Osborne Russell wrote of some of Jim Bridger's men who killed bull buffalo during the winter and discovered just how tough that meat could be. He wrote of the camp cook who poked the campfire with a club to remove the "ponderous mass of Bull beef." It was so tough it bounced five or six feet, like a huge rubber ball, ashes clinging to it, as the cook prepared it for carving (see *Journal of a Trapper,* ed. Aubrey L. Haines 39). Still others supplemented their diet with sourdough, which was often passed on to pioneers who arrived in this valley in the late 1800s.

The first settlers to bring wagons over Teton Pass would not have survived that first bitter winter without the help of earlier settlers, bachelors John Carnes, John Holland, John Cherry, and William Crawford. Many pioneer women had large families and ranch hands to feed. A housewife's ability to create a meal, often out of very little, was a mark of success. "These women," says Jean Stewart, "could take a rutabaga, carrot, potato, or an onion, and come up with something good to eat for their family. And a lot of times, they did that most of the winter."

For those who settled in the more agriculturally challenged places in Jackson Hole, food variety was severely restricted. Erma Chambers Nethercott was born and raised on a homestead in what is now the Elk Refuge. That rocky, infertile soil was so inhospitable that even indigenous wild hay didn't grow well there. That area came to be known as Poverty Flats, and sometimes its residents lived on the verge of starvation. Those pioneer women pushed their creativity to the limit. Of those tough times, Erma would later say, "We had to do the best we could with what we had. Even after we were married, we were so poor, all we had to eat was elk meat and onions for months at a time. We learned to serve it in a lot of different ways."

In the early days, there were no refrigerators, and even if there had been, there was no electricity to run them. Pioneers hung elk meat on the shady side of the house for the winter. When it was time to start dinner, they went outside and cut a slab of frozen meat to thaw. The noon meal, the largest of the day, was called dinner, and the night meal was called supper.

Peter Nelson family
(L-R: Almer Nelson, Acktor Nelson, Asker Nelson, Pearl Nelson (Deyo),
Emily Nelson (Coe), Peter Nelson, and Katrina Nelson)
Collection of the Jackson Hole Historical Society & Museum

Recipes and Baking

Jackson Hole pioneers had to be totally self-reliant. Housewives cooked on primitive wood stoves; oven temperatures were maintained by regularly adding pieces of wood of certain sizes and tested by how long the cook could stand to leave her hand inside the oven. In a Slow oven (200°-300°), the hand could be held inside the oven a full 60 seconds; in a Moderate oven (350°), 45 seconds; and in a Quick oven (400°-450°), only 35 seconds.

Pioneer women didn't use the same measurements we use today. When a recipe called for a tablespoon, the implement referred to might not have been a measuring spoon, but a large serving spoon. Several of these recipes call for a "good" Tablespoon of flour or salt. That was pioneer talk for "heaping." Because these women learned recipes from their mothers or from each other, if and when they wrote them down, they might include only sketchy directions. They assumed everyone knew butter and eggs were creamed together before

other ingredients were added to a cookie recipe. Unfortunately, even oven temperatures, though they were often hit and miss, sometimes were omitted. Occasionally, cooking times were not included. Some recipes were only a list of ingredients.

We hope you will not be too frustrated by the lack of directions in some of these old recipes. We believe they have merit and interest and, for the creative cook, can provide a culinary challenge.

This book also contains about 100 modern recipes reprinted from our weekly paper, *Teton Views,* volumes I and II. These recipes come from some of Jackson Hole's finest cooks. Some of them are descendants of early pioneer men and women who helped build this community. We have done our best to verify the accuracy of all recipes. If you have pioneer recipes you would like to share in a future volume, please let us know.

Pure Food Club Members
Back Row L To R: Amy Dallis, Christobel Kent, Mrs. T. Lloyd, Lucy Miner, Georgia (Ely) Crail, Etta Leek, Grandma Deloney.
Front Row: Grace Lloyd, Phoebe Beagle, Francis Deloney Clark, Calvin Beagle, Mrs. Charles Beagle, Mrs. Ely and Mrs. Hoagland
Photo taken by Stephen N. Leek sometime between 1929 and 1933.
Collection of the Jackson Hole Historical Society & Museum

The Pure Food Club of Jackson Hole

What was the Pure Food Club? Who belonged? What was its purpose? These questions have only partial answers, for, as far as we know, those who belonged to the club in the early 1900s are all gone. The written records we have seem to indicate that the club was more of a social unit, rather than an organization with a mission. While a report of one meeting stated that nutrition was discussed, the local paper detailed activities such as playing the card game 500. Although the group was undoubtedly interested in seeing that their families got "pure foods," more emphasis appeared to be given to their own refreshments. Perhaps the club was mostly an excuse to gather at each other's homes, to enjoy one another. In a day without television or even radio, people relied on each other for entertainment, and in this isolated community, getting together was vital for survival.

Evidence of the existence of the Pure Food Club of Jackson Hole has all but vanished. After extensive research, we found only two old-timers who remembered. Jean Stewart and Anna Ferrin remember, but even their recollections are sketchy. Jean's mother, Genevieve Van Vleck, belonged, and so did Dr. Charles Huff's wife, Edna.

In fact, probably most of the women who lived within the bounds of the Town of Jackson in the early 1900s belonged to the Pure Food Club, and membership undoubtedly extended to some who lived outside of town. Guests, including husbands and children, often were invited to functions.

The earliest scrap of written information we found about the club was a story in the March 15, 1917 issue of the *Jackson's Hole Courier:*

"Mr. and Mrs. S.N. Leek entertained at their home south of town on Saturday night the members of the Pure Food Club, together with their husbands and quite a number of additional guests, the company numbering nearly seventy-five. The trip to and from the ranch was made in sleighs, and since the evening was fine and the moon just right, the ride proved one of the enjoyable features of the evening." The group played 13 tables of Progressive High Five, using tally cards with photographs Stephen Leek himself had taken and then hand colored. Prizes were awarded to Mrs. Harry Wagner, Mr. R.E. Miller, Mrs. Richard Winger, and Mr. Oliver Reed. Following the games, refreshments were served. Later, musical numbers were performed by Mrs. Loomis, Mrs. Seelemire, and Mr. Dalley. Town librarian Mrs. Frank Tanner gave a reading.

It is likely that the Pure Food Club met twice a month. The next mention we found of their activities was in the March 14, 1918 issue of

the *Courier*. The club had met the previous Friday afternoon. Three sleigh loads of women, including guests, met at the home of Mrs. F.S. Wood east of Jackson. Club President, Mrs. Ely, presided over a business meeting. No one will ever know everything that was discussed that day, but the paper reported this tidbit:

"Among other things, it was decided at the meeting to limit the refreshments served at future meetings of the club; only one course may be served hereafter, at least during the period of the war.

"The balance of the afternoon was spent with conversation and sewing until, just before the guests departed for home, Mrs. Wood served a very enjoyable lunch." Mrs. E.P. Ellis was scheduled to entertain the club at the next meeting, which was scheduled for Friday afternoon, March 22, 1918, at the home of Mrs. Harry Wagner.

The May 13, 1920 *Courier* ran a short piece on the doings of the Pure Food Club, coincidentally, next to a story about the election of the town's first all-woman government. All elected candidates were members of the Pure Food Club, according to Jean Stewart. This club meeting was held at the home of the woman appointed by Mayor Grace Miller as town Health Officer—Edna Huff. Again, entertainment was the card game of 500. Mrs. Richard Winger and Mrs. D.C. Nowlin received prizes, and lunch was served. Mrs. M.D. Meeks was set to entertain at the next meeting, to be held at the Crabtree Hotel, owned by Henry Crabtree and his wife Rose, a newly elected city councilwoman.

The March 27, 1924 *Courier* gave a short report of the Pure Food Club meeting held the previous Friday at Mrs. H.M. Ely's home, with Mrs. Ed Mayer as associate hostess. At the 500 tables that day, Mrs. Harry Wagner and Mrs. John Thweatt received prizes. Apparently the rationing of the war was over by then, as "a very nice two-course luncheon was served, at the close of the games, by the hostesses, assisted by Mrs. Bruce Porter." The next meeting was scheduled for April 3, 1924, at the home of Mrs. Chas. Deloney. Hostess for the event was Mrs. Deloney's daughter, Mrs. Troy Pratt.

In the July 14, 1960 *Courier*, a photo of some members of the Pure Food Club was printed, showing about 20 women and children who had posed at the Redmond Ranch many years before. Among them were Mrs. O.E. Williams, Charlotte Lloyd, Mrs. Chas. Deloney, Mrs. Hambrick, Mrs. Maggie McBride, Mrs. Josephine Saunders, Mrs. Mae Deloney, Charlie Deloney, Mrs. Jessie Davina, Mrs. Jean Deloney Johnson, Mrs. Reata Griswold, Mrs. Charles Wort, Russell Wort, Mrs. T. Lloyd, Mrs. Tom Estes, Mrs. Steve Leek, Mrs. Charlie Beagle, Mrs. Vi Deloney Pratt, Lola May, and Mrs. Nancy Ely.

There's a reason those names sound familiar. Hundreds of people in the valley count them as their forebears, and they left a lasting legacy here in the Hole.

Jackson's All-Woman Government

In May 1920, Jackson Hole voters elected what many believe was the first all-woman town government in the world. Grace Miller, wife of Jackson State Bank president Robert Miller, was elected mayor. She defeated her opponent, Fred Lovejoy, by a two-to-one margin. Rose Crabtree, who ran against her own husband Henry, and Mae Deloney, both won two-year seats on the town council. Henry Crabtree later told reporters he held no ill will toward Rose. He felt that since she had done a good job of running the Crabtree Hotel, she was well qualified. He agreed that government was a woman's job, like housecleaning. Genevieve Van Vleck, the wife of Roy Van Vleck, who owned and operated Jackson Mercantile; and Faustina Haight, a schoolteacher, were both elected to one-year seats on the town council. The women met almost immediately to review town finances and make appointments. They appointed women to the other town positions. Marta Winger became clerk, Viola Lumbeck was treasurer, and Pearl Williams was town marshal. Pearl's salary was $40. Edna Huff, wife of the town doctor, was appointed health officer. She is referred to in many meeting minutes as "Mrs. Dr. Huff."

Reporters from around the country wrote stories about the change of political power in this little community, population about 300, and it became something of a flagship for those promoting women's rights. Although women in Wyoming had been voting since 1869, women nation-wide were just receiving the franchise in 1920, and political rights was a hot topic. Calvin Coolidge, Massachusetts governor at the time, congratulated Jackson on their "good sense." While some made much of the irony of this town, with its outlaw image, being governed by "petticoat rulers," Grace Miller played down this aspect, saying, "We were not campaigning for the office because we felt the need of pressing reforms. The voters of Jackson believe that women are not only entitled to equal suffrage, but they are also entitled to equality in the management of governmental affairs."

What really prompted the women to run was the condition of the town government. The women belonged to a social organization called the Pure Food Club, where they met to discuss nutrition and recipes, gossip, and play 500. It was here they began discussing the sad state of local politics. Men filled political offices reluctantly, and were reluctant to attend town council meetings after a long day's work in the fields or in their businesses. Many times, a vote couldn't be taken because a quorum wasn't present. Taxes and fines often went uncollected. According to some accounts, when the female administration took over,

the town coffers contained only about $200. Pigs and cattle rooted and grazed in the town square and surrounding areas. Jean Stewart, daughter of councilwoman Genevieve Van Vleck, said young people hired to watch the town herd often grazed them in the cemetery on the hillside south of town. The spot had no fence, and since the town didn't officially own the cemetery property, there was no way of building one. The women agreed that cows grazing among the dead was a disgrace. And that wasn't the only problem with the cemetery. Only a steep, winding trail led to the burial sites. In winter, it was nearly impossible to carry caskets through the deep snow, and in summer, dust and heat made travel almost as miserable. According to Jean Stewart, sometimes bodies were stored through the winter and buried after the weather improved.

Newspaperwoman Cissy Patterson, known in these parts as the Countess of Flat Creek, wrote in the *Omaha World Herald* of the Jackson women's political victory. Her story quoted councilwoman Rose Crabtree, who didn't mince words about the problems Jackson faced: "The men had made just a mess of running this town. Seven hundred and fifty dollars in debt and nothing to show for it. Keeping a little town like Jackson is like keeping house. We women who were elected are all good housekeepers. Whoever heard of a good man housekeeper? Why, look at the old bachelors around here. Most of them live like wild animals. As for cooking, all they know is how to open a tin can into a frying pan.

"Now, in Jackson, the men did the foolishest things. They built a two-foot ditch all through town, and put up one-foot culverts. Consequently our streets are flooded half the time. We women are goin' to have a town well before next year, too. It's all right in summer; we get our water from the irrigating ditches, but in the winter every drop used in this place has to be hauled in barrels from the river through the ice and snow. Did you ever hear of anything so ridiculous?"

"And we're going to level the grade to the cemetery. That's for sure. The way they've got it, the corpse has to be carried half a mile up the hill to be buried—wagons and cars can't make it in bad weather. Like as not, the men thought the corpse would oblige by getting out and walking just a little way."

The water system and cemetery weren't the only things the women wanted to fix. The previous garbage collector had simply picked up refuse from one home and then dumped it again on any

convenient vacant lot. The women initiated formal garbage collection and a disposal site, making it a misdemeanor to put garbage on city streets or in vacant lots. They fined owners of pigs, cows, dogs, and horses left loose on the streets. And they collected the fines, along with overdue taxes, sometimes even visiting folks who were delinquent, shaming them into paying up. Within two weeks, the town treasury had risen to $2,000, and they began spending it on improvements right away. They built the first boardwalks, graded town streets, and organized a town clean-up week, a tradition that continues today. They passed ordinances against firecrackers and explosives and began to address the problem of "annoying engine exhaust." They installed new culverts into irrigation ditches and began studies for a town water system. They installed street lights and contracted with Ed Benson to place poles for power lines.

As early as June 14, 1920, they began negotiations to secure title to the 40-acre cemetery, and they continued until they purchased the site. In the early part of 1921, they bought a strip of land for $150 from George Kelly to provide a road to the cemetery. In April, they paid him $10 for snow removal. Their yearly salaries were $25 for mayor, $20 for councilwomen, $25 for health officer, and $100 for clerk.

Millor, Van Vlcck, and I laight were all re-elected in 1921, this time by a vote of three to one. The women's government continued until 1923, when they decided not to run again, perhaps thinking they had pretty much completed their agenda and their households needed more attention. In summing up their accomplishments, Grace Miller told one reporter: "We simply tried to work together. We put into practice the same thrifty principles we exercise in our homes. We wanted a clean, well-kept, progressive town in which to raise our families. What is good government but a breeding-place for good citizenship?"

Author's note:

In the past few weeks, my collaborator and dear friend, Jean Van Vleck Stewart, passed away. Many of Jean's stories and family recipes are preserved herein. This book would never have been written without her help. In real sense, it is Jean's book.

—Judy S. Clayton, April 9, 2001

Table of Contents

Appetizers, Beverages & Breakfast Dishes

Thirsty picnickers

Collection of the Jackson Hole Historical Society & Museum

38140-ca-1

Albert Nelson, Sr., Wyoming's first game warden

Photo courtesy Anna Nelson Ferrin

38140-ca-1b

Appetizers, Beverages & Breakfast Dishes

Appetizers

FRUIT DIP

Susan May
Jackson Hole resident since 1975

1 8-oz. pkg. cream cheese (not low fat)
1 small jar of marshmallow creme

melon, strawberries, grapes, and/or other fruits

Let cream cheese warm to room temperature. Mix well with marshmallow creme and refrigerate. Serve with fruit.

Recipe Note: Susan got this recipe from a cousin. It makes an elegant dip for summertime parties. Susan's husband, Les May, was born and raised in Jackson Hole. He owns and operates Western Heritage Builders.

HOT CHEESE BEAN DIP

Jett Thompson
Jackson Hole resident since 1970

1 large can chili
1 can cream of Mushroom soup
1 lb. grated cheddar cheese

1 chopped onion
crushed corn chips

Mix chilli, soup, onion, and cheese together in large casserole dish. Top with crushed chips. Bake at 350° for one hour. Serve with chips.

Recipe Note: Jett and husband George Thompson have seven grown children. George is a partner in Thompson, Palmer & Associates. This simple recipe is great for parties and potluck dinners.

"A generation which ignores history has no past - and no future."
- Robert A. Heinlein

THREE-POUND PARTY DIP

Tom Caruso
Jackson Hole resident since 1990s

1 lb. hamburger
1 lb. ground Italian sausage
1 lb. Velveeta cheese

1 8-oz. can Ortega medium hot
salsa with onions and peppers

Brown hamburger and sausage together. Drain. Cut up and add Velveeta cheese to meat mixture. Let cheese melt, and mix in salsa. When mixture is warm through, serve with tortilla corn chips.

Recipe Note: Tom created this recipe himself. It's a great treat for football or poker games.

Beverages

GINGER BEER
(A non-alcoholic beverage)

Happy Chambers Weston
Jackson Hole resident since she was 5 years old

fresh ginger root the size of
  your thumb
2 qt. boiling water
1 c. sugar

1 tsp. cream of tartar
1 lemon, squeezed
1 tsp. dry yeast

Smash the ginger root (one good whack with a rolling pin), and add it to boiling water, along with the lemon juice and sugar. When mixture cools to lukewarm, add yeast and cream of tartar. Stir until yeast dissolves. Cover and let stand overnight. In the morning, pour liquid into clean bottles and cork. Leave sediment in pan. Let bottles stand at room temperature 3-4 days until fermented. Chill, then enjoy. Don't allow to ferment too long, or beverage will blow its cork. Check after 2 days to see if it's bubbly. Chill when it reaches this stage.

Recipe Note: Happy Weston, Vice President of Wilson Homemakers, got this recipe from a friend's old cookbook. Happy's grandfather, Ed Chambers homesteaded near the Practice Rocks by Blacktail Butte.

38140-01

Breakfast Dishes

WAFFLES

Genevieve Van Vleck
Member of the Pure Food Club

2 c. flour
4 tsp. baking powder
½ tsp. salt
2 tsp. sugar

1¾ c. milk
2 eggs, separated
½ c. melted butter

Sift together flour, baking powder, salt, and sugar. Mix milk with beaten egg yolks. Add melted butter. Then add dry ingredients to milk, egg yolk, and butter mixture. Fold in beaten egg whites. Cook on waffle iron until done.

Recipe Note: Genevieve Van Vleck and her husband Roy were owners of one of Jackson's earliest stores, the Jackson Mercantile. Genevieve was part of the all-woman government in Jackson in the early 1920s. This recipe is shared by her daughter, Jean Stewart.

OVERNIGHT APPLE FRENCH TOAST

Jackie Richardson
Jackson Hole resident since 1972

1 c. packed brown sugar
½ c. butter
2 tsp. light corn syrup
3 eggs
2 large Granny Smith apples

1 c. milk
1 tsp. vanilla
9 slices French bread, ¾-inch
thick, day old

Syrup ingredients:

1 c. applesauce
1 10-oz. jar apple jelly

½ tsp. cinnamon
½ tsp. ground cloves

In a small pan, cook brown sugar, butter, and syrup until thick, about 5 minutes. Pour into ungreased 9 x 13 inch baking pan. Arrange peeled apple slices on top of "caramel" on pan bottom. In a bowl, beat eggs, milk, and vanilla. Dip bread slices into the mixture for 1 minute, and place bread slices on top of apples. Pour any remaining mixture over bread. Cover and refrigerate overnight. Remove from refrigerator 30 minutes before baking; then bake uncovered at 350° for 35-40 minutes. Combine syrup ingredients in a medium saucepan, stirring frequently until hot. Serve over French toast.

Recipe Note: Jackie and husband Weldon Richardson own and operate the Huff House Inn Bed and Breakfast, the former home of Pure Food Club member Edna Huff. This recipe is a favorite of their guests. Jackie says this French toast is also good topped by a dollop of vanilla yogurt.

FRIED CAKES

Lenora Lloyd
Member of the Pure Food Club

1 egg, beaten very light	1 c. sour milk
1 c. sugar	1 tsp. salt
2 T. sour cream or melted butter	1 tsp. soda
1 T. brandy	

Beat egg, sugar, sour cream, and brandy. Then add sour milk, salt, and soda. Mix lightly, and fry in grease on hot griddle. This recipe appears to lack flour. Try it at your own risk!

Recipe Note: Lenora Lloyd was postmistress of Jackson for years during the 1920s and 30s. Her husband, Butch, was the town butcher. He often had a stogie in his mouth as he served up housewives' meat orders. The Lloyds were related to the Steve Leek family.

COCONUT BRUNCH

Jackie Richardson
Jackson Hole resident since 1972

4 eggs	3 c. all-purpose flour
2 c. granulated white sugar	2 tsp. vanilla
1 c. salad oil	½ tsp. baking powder
½ tsp. baking soda	1 c. buttermilk
½ tsp. salt	1 c. chopped nuts
1 c. coconut	

Beat eggs until thick and lemon colored. Add sugar, oil, and vanilla. Blend well. Sift dry ingredients together. Add to egg mixture alternately with buttermilk. Then fold in coconut and nuts. Pour into greased 10-inch tube pan. Bake at 325° about one hour. Before removing cake from oven, bring to a boil 1 cup sugar with ½ cup water and 2 Tablespoons butter or margarine. Pour this mixture over the hot cake, and let it cool in the pan for two hours. Then turn it upside down onto a plate to finish cooling and absorb the syrup.

Recipe Note: This recipe is a favorite of guests at the Richardsons' Huff House Inn Bed & Breakfast, currently located in the former home of Pure Food Club member Edna Huff and husband Dr. Charles Huff.

"For some life lasts a short while, but the memories it holds last forever."
- Laura Swenson

MEXICAN EGG BREAKFAST CASSEROLE

Sherry Blair Daigle
Jackson Hole native

1 lb. ground bulk breakfast
   sausage
½ lb. grated cheddar cheese
½ lb. grated Monterey Jack
   cheese
1 sm. onion, minced
1 sm. pepper (red or green),
   minced

6 eggs
1 c. canned milk
3 T. flour
any type of salsa (Sherry uses
   green chile.)

Preheat oven to 350°. Brown sausage and layer in bottom of 9 x 12-inch pan. Layer minced onion and pepper on top of sausage. Mix cheeses together, and layer on top of peppers and onions. Beat eggs, milk, and flour together and pour over cheese layer. Bake 35-40 minutes. Remove from oven, and pour salsa over top. Let stand 15 minutes before serving.

Recipe Note: Sherry Blair Daigle is the daughter of Calvin and Virginia Blair and the granddaughter of LaPreal and the late Lew Blair. An excellent cook, she is presently serving as Teton County Clerk.

FARMER'S CASSEROLE

Jackie Richardson
Jackson Hole resident since 1972

3 c. shredded frozen or fresh
   hash brown potatoes
¾ c. Monterey Jack cheese with
   jalapeño peppers, grated
1 c. fully cooked ham or
   Canadian bacon, chopped

¼ c. sliced green onions
1 12-oz. can evaporated milk
⅛ tsp. salt
4 eggs
¼ tsp. pepper

Grease 2-quart square baking dish. Arrange potatoes evenly in bottom of dish. Sprinkle with cheese, ham, and onions. Mix eggs, milk, salt and pepper; and pour over potatoes. Bake uncovered at 350° for 40-45 minutes. Can be made ahead, refrigerated, and baked the next day. If chilled overnight, bake for 55-60 minutes.

Recipe Note: Jackie got this recipe from Jeannie Ferrin who operated the Inn at Buffalo Fork Bed and Breakfast. It is a favorite of Jackie's B & B guests.

UP ALL NIGHT COFFEE CAKE

Nancy Dunham
Jackson Hole resident since 1974

¾ c. chopped nuts
20-22 frozen Rhodes dinner rolls
1 3¼-oz. pkg. instant or regular
   butterscotch pudding mix

½ c. brown sugar
½ c. butter or margarine, melted
cinnamon to taste

Grease a bundt pan and sprinkle nuts on bottom of pan. Arrange rolls evenly over nuts. Sprinkle dry pudding mix over rolls. In small bowl, combine sugar and cinnamon. Cover rolls with sugar mixture. Pour melted margarine or butter over sugar mixture. Place in cold oven to remain overnight. In the morning, remove rolls from oven and preheat oven to 350°. Return rolls to oven and bake for 25 minutes or until brown. Remove from oven and turn out of pan.

Recipe Note: Nancy and Tom Dunham have three children. They have both worked in the Teton County School District for many years. Tom is a local meteorologist. "This recipe is easy and very good," Nancy says. "That's the kind I like."

BAKED APRICOTS

Jolynn Coonce
Jackson Hole resident since 1958

2 28-oz. cans apricots, drained
2 c. light brown sugar
1 12-oz. box Ritz crackers,
   crumbled

1 cube butter or margarine

In a large casserole dish, make one layer of cracker crumbs; then one of brown sugar; then one of the butter, sliced into pats; then one of apricots. Repeat until all ingredients are used, usually twice. Bake at 300° for 50 minutes, covered, then another 10 minutes, uncovered.

Recipe Note: Jolynn uses this recipe she got from her sister-in-law as a breakfast casserole, served with baked eggs. It's easy and tastes great. Jolynn's late husband, Jim, taught school in Jackson Hole for 20 years. Jolynn is currently serving as a Teton County Commissioner.

"When one door closes, another opens. But we often look so regretfully upon the closed door that we don't see the one that has opened for us."
- Alexander Graham Bell

38140-01

Breads & Rolls

Lunch on the road

Bruce Porter Collection, Jackson Hole Historical Society & Museum

38140-ca-2

Grade School hot lunch cooks
Anna Ferrin and Daisy Bush

Photo courtesy Anna Nelson Ferrin

38140-ca-2b

Breads & Rolls

Breads

MUFFINS

Georgia Ely
Member of the Pure Food Club

½ c. sugar
¼ c. butter
3 eggs
1 c. sweet milk

2 c. flour
2 tsp. baking powder
pinch of salt

Beat sugar, butter and eggs in mixing bowl. Mix in milk. Sift together flour, baking powder and salt, and add to mixing bowl. Spoon into greased muffin tins until ¾ full. Bake at 375° for 12-15 minutes.

Recipe Note: Georgia Ely lived close to Genevieve Van Vleck and often sewed for her.

MEXICAN CORN BREAD

Marge Ryan
Jackson Hole native, born on Mormon Row

1 c. margarine
1 c. flour
1 c. sugar
1 c. cornmeal
4 eggs
4 tsp. baking powder

½ tsp. salt
1 4-oz. can of chopped green chilies
1 1-lb. can of cream style corn
1 c. shredded jack and cheddar cheese

Cream margarine and sugar. Add eggs, one at a time, mixing well. Add chilies, corn, and cheese. Mix well. Sift and mix in dry ingredients well. Bake at 300° in 9 x 13-inch pan for 1 hour.

Recipe Note: Marge and husband John Ryan have both lived here all their lives. Marge is an excellent cook. She worked for the local phone company and for Jackson Drug. She recently retired as Teton County Elections Clerk. She doesn't remember where she got this delicious recipe, but it's a family favorite.

COCOA BREAD

Edna Huff
Member of the Pure Food Club

½ c. lukewarm water
2 T. sugar
2 yeast cakes
2 c. milk
1 scant c. sugar

⅔ c. cocoa
3 T. shortening
2 tsp. salt
6+ c. flour

Add 2 tablespoons sugar to ½ c. lukewarm water. Add 2 yeast cakes (or 2 pkgs. yeast), and set aside. Scald milk with 1 scant cup sugar mixed with cocoa. Add shortening and salt. Mix well. Pour into mixing bowl and set aside until luke warm. Add yeast mixture and 4 cups of flour. Beat well. Add 2 cups more flour, more if needed to make bread dough consistency. Knead until smooth and elastic, adding more flour as necessary. Let rise until double in bulk. Knead slightly and shape into loaves. Put into greased bread pans or B.K. cans (cans baking powder came in, probably about the size of tomato juice cans today). Let rise again until double in bulk. Start baking in moderate oven at 350° if not raising as high as you'd like. If it is light, bake at 450°. Increase or decrease oven temperatures between 350° and 450° while baking. Bake 40 minutes in B. K. cans or 45 minutes in bread pans.

Recipe Note: Edna Huff was married to Jackson's country doctor, Charles Huff. She was Health Officer during the town's all-woman administration between 1920 and 1923. This recipe was in Genevieve Van Vleck's hand-written cookbook and was shared by Genevieve's daughter, Jean Stewart.

"Wheresoever you go, go with all your heart."

- Confucius

38140-01

COCONUT BREAD

Edna Caresia
Jackson Hole resident since 1971

2 c. sugar
1 c. cooking oil
4 eggs
2 tsp. coconut flavoring
1/2 tsp. baking powder
1 c. buttermilk

1 c. coconut
1 c. chopped nuts
3 c. flour
1/2 tsp. soda
1/2 tsp. salt

Mix well sugar, oil, and eggs. Combine flour, soda, baking powder, and salt. Add to oil mixture alternately with buttermilk. Add coconut flavoring, coconut, and nuts. Bake in greased and floured pans for 1 hour at 325°. When done, punch holes in top of bread with toothpick.

Glaze:

1 T. margarine
1/2 c. sugar

1/2 tsp. coconut flavoring
1/4 c. water

Melt margarine in pan. Blend in sugar, coconut flavoring, and water. Heat until sugar is dissolved. While bread is hot, pour over top.

Recipe Note: Edna got this recipe from one of her daughters-in-law and has used it for holiday desserts and potluck dinners. Edna's husband Fred is retired from the National Park Service, and Edna is retired from the Teton County Clerk's Office.

HOMEMADE WHOLE WHEAT BREAD

Delar Cheney
Sporadic Jackson Hole resident since 1959

1 c. water
3 T. yeast
1 tsp. sugar
13 c. water

1 c. oil
1 c. honey
1 heaping T. salt
whole-wheat flour

Mix together 1 cup water, yeast, and sugar. Allow yeast to work about 10 minutes. In a large mixing bowl, add 13 cups water, oil, honey, and salt. Mix well. Add yeast mixture and enough whole-wheat flour (freshly ground if possible) to make a stiff dough. If dough isn't stiff enough, the center of loaves will cave in. Knead until dough is satiny. Let rise 10-15 minutes. Punch down and form into loaves. Place in well greased loaf pans. Let rise about 1/2 hour or until loaves are just above the top of pans. This recipe makes about nine loaves. Bake at 300° about 1 hour and 10 minutes. Be sure loaves are browned and done before removing from oven.

Recipe Note: Delar got this recipe from a bread machine company and made improvements and adaptations. He has been making bread for more than 10 years. He and his wife LaDawn recently moved to Idaho.

NUT BREAD

Grace Miller
Member of the Pure Food Club

1 c. sugar
1 egg
3 scant tsp. baking powder

1 c. milk
3 c. flour
1 c. nuts

Mix all ingredients together, place in greased loaf pans. Raise 40 minutes and bake 40 minutes. This old recipe had no baking temperature. Try baking at 350° until cake tests done.

Recipe Note: Grace Miller and husband Robert homesteaded much of what is now the National Elk Refuge. She was elected Jackson Town mayor in 1920 and served for three years. This recipe, taken from an old cookbook is somewhat incomplete. Try it at your own risk!

POPPYSEED BREAD

Linda Drumm
Moved to Jackson Hole in 1997

3 c. all-purpose flour
1½ tsp. baking powder
1⅛ c. vegetable oil
2¼ c. sugar
1½ tsp. vanilla extract

1½ tsp. salt
3 eggs
1½ c. milk
3 T. poppy seeds
1½ tsp. almond extract

Combine flour, salt, and baking powder. In separate bowl, combine eggs, oil, milk, and sugar. Add dry ingredients to liquid, and mix well. Add poppy seeds, vanilla, and almond extracts. Pour into two greased and floured loaf pans. Bake at 325° for 45 minutes.

Glaze:

1 c. confectioners' sugar
¾ tsp. vanilla

3 tsp. lemon juice
¾ tsp. almond extract

Put all ingredients into small microwaveable bowl. Microwave until warm, stirring occasionally. Punch holes into warm bread with a fork, and pour warm glaze over bread. Cool. Remove bread from pans, and serve.

Recipe Note: Linda Drumm and husband Michael moved here to open Last Flight Out, a retail store. They have since moved from the valley. Linda is an excellent cook and has won many recipe contests. Her family loves this sweet bread.

WHOLE WHEAT BREAD

Susie Nethercott
Jackson Hole native

2 T. yeast
½ c. very warm water
5 c. very hot water
⅔ c. canola oil

⅓ c. honey
⅓ c. Black Strap Molasses
2 T. salt
up to 10 c. whole-wheat flour

In small bowl, sprinkle yeast over ½ cup very warm water. Let work 10 minutes. Meanwhile, pour 5 cups very hot water in a large mixing bowl. Add oil, honey, molasses, and salt. Stirring continually, add 3 cups flour, one at a time. Then pour yeast mixture into mixing bowl. Stir, and continue to add from 5 to 7 more cups of whole-wheat flour. Mix well. You may not need all 10 cups of flour; just add enough to make the mixture elastic. Knead 5 minutes, sprinkling flour on counter top as you knead. Divide dough into fourths, form each into a loaf, and place in four medium-sized greased bread pans. Let rise 30-40 minutes. Bake 30-35 minutes at 350°.

Recipe Note: Susie got this recipe from Betty Perkinson, a former neighbor, many years ago. It always works and has become a family staple.

FRIED CAKES
(Real Doughnuts)

Georgia Ely
Member of the Pure Food Club

1 c. sponge (sourdough)
1 beaten egg
½ c. sugar
good-sized piece of melted
  shortening

flavoring
flour

Mix sponge with egg, sugar, melted shortening and flavoring if desired. Add enough flour to make a soft dough. Let it rise in a warm place. When it is nice and puffy, you roll it and roll out. Then cut into doughnuts, and let them rise. Then drop in hot fat and fry.

Recipe Note: Georgia Ely made excellent doughnuts. This recipe may be somewhat incomplete, so augment it with instructions from a more modern cookbook source before trying it out.

MORNING GLORY MUFFINS

Joyce Sawczuk
Jackson Hole resident since 1993

4 c. shredded carrots	1 tsp. vanilla
2 apples, shredded	1¾ to 2½ c. sugar
1 c. pecans, chopped	4 c. flour
1 c. raisins	4 tsp. cinnamon
1 c. coconut, shredded	4 tsp. baking soda
6 eggs	1 tsp. salt
1½-2 c. vegetable oil	

Combine and mix well: carrots, apples, pecans, raisins, coconut, eggs, vegetable oil, and vanilla. Sift together sugar, flour, cinnamon, baking soda, and salt. Then add to first mixture, stirring well. Spoon dough into greased muffin tins, and bake at 375° for 20 minutes or until done.

Recipe Note: Joyce is Office Manager for the Jackson Hole Historical Society & Museum. This recipe makes a large batch of filling, delicious muffins. Joyce, who enjoys cooking for family and friends, got this recipe years ago from her sister.

"Time is like an addiction, you always want more."

- Scott Ishman

38140-01

DOUBLE BUTTERSCOTCH CRESCENT ROLLS

Pat Weber
Jackson Hole resident since 1968

Rolls:

1 pkg. dry yeast
1¼ c. warm water
1 3-oz. pkg. instant butterscotch
  pudding mix
1½ c. milk

½ c. melted butter
2 eggs
2 tsp. salt
4½-5½ c. flour

Filling:

¼ c. melted butter
⅔ c. brown sugar
2 T. flour

⅔ c. grated coconut
⅓ c. pecan pieces

Glaze:

½ c. brown sugar
2 T. water

2 T. butter
1 c. powdered sugar

Soften yeast in warm water. Prepare pudding mix, using 1½ c. milk. When thickened, add melted butter. Blend unbeaten eggs, salt, and softened yeast into pudding. Gradually add flour to form a stiff dough, beating well after each addition. Cover and let rise in a warm place about 1½ hours. For filling, combine melted butter, brown sugar, flour, coconut, and pecan pieces. Divide dough into thirds and roll each part into a 15-inch circle. Cut each circle of dough into 12 wedges, using a pastry wheel. Place rounded teaspoon of filling onto each wedge and roll up, starting with the wide end. Place on cookie sheet in crescent form. Let rise in warm place about 1 hour. Bake at 375° for 12-15 minutes. For glaze, combine brown sugar, water, and butter in saucepan. Bring to boil, and boil one minute. Stir in powdered sugar and thin with milk if necessary. Glaze rolls while still warm. Makes 3 dozen rolls.

Recipe Note: Pat and Jack Weber have operated Weber Drilling for more than 33 years. Pat got this delicious recipe from the Casper Star Tribune.

"Keep your face to the sunshine and you cannot see the shadows."
- Helen Keller

Recipe Favorites

38140-01

Soups, Salads & Vegetables

Cowboy Bar, Moore's Cafe, Jewelry Store, early 1930s

Collection of the Jackson Hole Historical Society & Museum

An outdoor dinner at the Moosehead Ranch

Collection of the Jackson Hole Historical Society & Museum

38140-ca-3b

Soups, Salads & Vegetables

Soups

NORTH CAROLINA BRUNSWICK STEW

Lokey Lytjen
Jackson Hole resident since 1993

1 chicken, skinned as much as possible
2 large cans tomatoes
1 can tomato paste
2 cans creamed corn

5 to 7 potatoes
2 lg. onions
Seasonings of your choice
potato flakes for thickening

Boil chicken. Debone and string meat. Finely dice potatoes and onions. Boil together with chicken meat and stock in a large pot until tender. Add tomatoes, tomato paste, and corn to potatoes and onions and stock. Season with salt, pepper, some cayenne pepper, a little Tabasco, a little Lea and Perrins, or whatever you prefer. Simmer for a good while, 30-45 minutes. Thicken to desired consistency with instant mashed potato flakes. You may add butter beans if you like. This dish is excellent served with a salad and French bread or corn bread.

Recipe Note: In both Georgia and North Carolina, this dish traditionally accompanies barbecue. Lokey grew up eating Brunswick Stew. She is Executive Director of the Jackson Hole Historical Society & Museum.

POTATO SOUP

Genevieve Van Vleck
Member of the Pure Food Club

3 potatoes
1 qt. milk
2 slices of onion
2 to 4 T. butter
2 T. flour
1½ T. salt

¼ T. celery salt
⅛ T. pepper
few grains of Cayenne
1 T. chopped parsley
1 qt. milk or water

Cook potatoes in boiling salted water with onion. When soft, push through a strainer. Make a thickening with butter and flour. Heat 2 quarts milk or 1 quart milk and 1 quart water. Stir in strained potatoes and thickening. Add seasonings. Garnish with chopped parsley and serve.

Recipe Note: Genevieve Van Vleck got this recipe from her mother in Michigan before she moved here. Her daughter, Jean Stewart says, "Grandmother was a little worried about Mother when she got married. Dad was really skinny, so Grandmother wrote down some recipes for her."

TACO SOUP

Anna Bush
Jackson Hole native

1 lb. hamburger
1 lg. onion, chopped
1 15-oz. can kidney beans with juice
1 15-oz. can whole tomatoes, diced

1 15-oz. can whole kernel corn with juice
1 8-oz. can tomato sauce
2 c. water
1 pkg. taco seasoning

In bottom of kettle, brown hamburger and onion. Drain. Add all other ingredients, and bring to a boil. Simmer, covered, for 20 minutes.

Recipe Note: Anna Bush works for her mother Clara at Gai Mode Beauty Salon. Anna's great-grandparents, T.A. and Lucile Moulton, homesteaded on Mormon Row. This recipe came from Anna's sisters and has become a family staple. It can be garnished with grated cheese, sour cream, and/or taco chips.

RANCHER SOUP

Dene Beesley
Moved to Jackson Hole in 1954

1 lb. ground beef
1 medium green pepper, chopped
1 envelope onion soup mix
2 16-oz. cans of tomatoes
2½ c. water

2 medium carrots, diced
2 medium potatoes, diced
¼ c. barley
1½ tsp. chili powder
½ c. celery, sliced

Brown meat and drain off fat. Add soup mix, tomatoes, barley, water, and chili powder. Bring to a boil. Add fresh vegetables and simmer till done.

Recipe Note: Dene Beesley and husband Dell owned and operated a freight business and later a dry cleaning operation in Jackson. This recipe is a favorite for cool fall days. Dene and Dell moved to Utah in recent years.

"Life moves pretty fast. If you don't stop and look around once in a while, you could miss it."

- Ferris Bueller

QUICK MINESTRONE SOUP

Dene Beesley
Jackson Hole resident since 1954

1 pkg. frozen Italian vegetables
1/2 lb. lean ground beef
  (browned and drained)
2 cans Swanson Chicken Broth
1/3 c. catsup
1/2 c. small egg noodles (not
  Chinese)

2 T. celery leaves
2 T. dry minced onion
Good Season brand Italian salad
  dressing

Blend celery (can use celery and leaves, add more if desired) and onions in blender with chicken broth. Mix all ingredients in large saucepan, and add salad dressing 1 Tablespoon at a time, to taste. Left-over cooked vegetables can also be added. Simmer 30 minutes.

Recipe Note: Dene and Dell Beesley have four children and seven grandchildren, some of whom still live in the valley. Dene and Dell moved to Utah in recent years, but keep in close contact with friends and family here. Dene got this recipe from her sister. It's a great way to transform leftovers into a new dish.

IN A STEW OVER YOU

Carol Richardson
Jackson Hole resident for more than 20 years

6 slices bacon
1 c. diced celery
1 lb. hamburger or stew meat,
  cut in small pieces
1 large can of tomato juice
1 pkg. brown gravy mix

1/2 c. chopped carrots
2 c. sliced potatoes
1 can whole kernel corn
1 c. chopped onion
1/2 c. chopped green pepper

Cook bacon until crisp. Drain, crumble. and set aside. Sauté onions and green pepper in bacon grease. Add meat. Cook well. Add celery, tomato juice, gravy mix, carrots, potatoes, and corn. Simmer on low heat for 1 1/2 to 2 hours, stirring often. Check for doneness of potatoes. Sprinkle with bacon before serving.

Recipe Note: Carol has served on the Jackson Town Council. She brought this recipe with her from Texas when she moved to the valley.

VEGETABLE BEEF SOUP

Colleen Fisher
Jackson Hole resident since 1965

2 beef bones from a steak or roast, with some meat on them
1 2-lb. chuck roast, washed and cut in large pieces
4 whole bay leaves
1 tsp. Accent (opt.)
3/4 tsp. powdered smoke seasoning
1 tsp. Gourmet seasoning (opt.)
salt and pepper
1 qt. tomato juice
1 packet Instant Cream of Wheat
1 large onion, chopped
4 big celery stalks with leaves, chopped
5 garlic cloves, chopped (opt.)
4 lg. carrots, sliced
6 red potatoes, peeled and quartered
1 green pepper, sliced and chopped
1/4-1/2 head of cabbage, cut in wedges
2 c. fresh green beans with ends and strings removed
2 zucchini, chunked
1 or more ears of corn, husked

Place bones, roast, bay leaves, and seasonings (to taste) in a large stew pot, and cover with water. Bring to a boil, turn to low heat, and simmer until meat is almost done, about 2 hours. When liquid has boiled down, add another 2 c. water or more as needed and 1 qt. tomato juice. Thicken with 1 packet Instant Cream of Wheat, diluted with about 1 c. water to desired thickness. Stir occasionally. Then add onion, celery, and garlic. Next, add carrots, red potatoes, green pepper, cabbage, fresh green beans, and zucchini. Place ears of corn on top of stew (opt.) Return to boil and simmer until all vegetables are tender. When stew is ready, be sure to remove all bay leaves before serving. Corn ears can be eaten just as cooked and seasoned by the stew or can be buttered for additional flavor.

Recipe Note: Colleen Fisher passed away in 1999. She was a wonderful cook. She and husband Don had five children. She loved to cook and share her creations. This hearty recipe is great for those cold winter nights in the valley.

To be a star, you must shine your own light, follow your own path and don't worry about the darkness for that is when stars shine the brightest.
- Unknown

38140-01

OLD BRUNSWICK STEW

Happy Chambers Weston
Jackson Hole resident since she was 5 years old

whole chicken	5 potatoes
6 tomatoes, cut up	½ pt. butter beans
4 ears of corn, scraped from cob	salt and pepper

Boil chicken until meat is tender and falls off the bone, remove bones. Add to chicken and broth tomatoes, corn, potatoes, butter beans, and salt and pepper. Put it in at an early hour, and let it stew until it becomes thick.

Recipe Note: Happy Weston got this old pioneer stew from her friend's cookbook. It was first published in an early 1800s cookbook. This stew was originally made from squirrel meat, but chicken will substitute. Happy is Vice President of Wilson Homemakers.

"Every day is a good day."

- Yun-Men

Salads

PRETZEL SALAD

Pat Weber
Jackson Hole resident since 1968

Crust:

2 c. crushed pretzels   1 T. sugar
¾ c. margarine, melted

Filling:

1 8-oz. pkg. cream cheese   1 c. sugar
1 4-oz. container frozen whipped
  dessert topping, thawed

Topping:

2 c. pineapple juice   2 10-oz. pkgs. frozen
2 3-oz. pkgs. strawberry gelatin   strawberries

Combine crushed pretzels and 1 T. sugar. Add margarine, stirring until well combined. Press onto bottom of a 9 x 13-inch baking pan, at least 2 inches deep. Bake in a 350° oven 6-10 minutes; cool. Beat together cream cheese and 1 cup sugar till smooth. Fold in whipped dessert topping. Spread mixture over cooled crust. Combine pineapple juice and strawberry gelatin in a small saucepan. Cook over medium heat till gelatin is dissolved. Add strawberries. Pour gelatin mixture over cream cheese layer. Cover and chill 6 hours or overnight. Cut into squares to serve. Makes 15 servings.

Recipe Note: Pat and husband Jack Weber have owned and operated Weber Drilling in Jackson Hole for more than 30 years. Pat is an excellent cook. This recipe can be considered either a salad or a dessert and is great for potluck dinners.

CHICKEN SALAD WITH BUTTER BEANS AND GRAPES

Donna Shindurling
Jackson Hole resident for many years

1/4 c. mayonnaise
1 tsp. dried mint leaves
1/4 tsp. pepper
2 T. lemon juice
3/4 tsp. salt
8 oz. cooked chicken bits (1 1/2 c.)

1 can butter beans, rinsed and drained
1 1/4 c. seedless red grapes, cut in half or whole
1 1/4 c. diced, unpeeled cucumber or other fresh vegetables

Whisk in a large salad bowl: mayonnaise, mint leaves, pepper, lemon juice, and salt. Add chicken, beans, grapes, and cucumber. Stir to coat with dressing.

Recipe Note: You may substitute Brianna's Home Style Dressing with Poppy Seeds for the above dressing mixture. The recipe can be extended by adding more dressing and cooked pasta. Donna Shindurling taught school at Wilson many years ago. She and husband Bud have moved from the valley.

FRUIT SALAD DRESSING

Charlene Bressler
Jackson Hole native

3 eggs
4 T. flour
1/2 c. sugar
1 tsp. salt
1/4 tsp. white pepper

1/4 tsp. mustard
1/2 c. vinegar
1/2 c. water
2 T. butter

Beat eggs and add flour, sugar, salt, pepper, and mustard. Add the rest of the ingredients and cook in a double boiler until thick and creamy. Stir frequently to prevent lumping. This dressing can be thinned with sweet, sour, or whipped cream and served on head lettuce or fruit salads.

Recipe Note: This recipe is reprinted from the newspaper clipping recipe collection of Charlene Bressler.

MIXED-GRAIN SALAD WITH DRIED FRUIT

Susan Chambers
Jackson Hole resident for many years

¹/₄ c. vegetable oil
¹/₂ c. chopped shallots
1 c. brown rice
1 c. wild rice
1 c. wheat berries
2 c. water
2 c. chicken stock or canned
  low-salt chicken broth

³/₄ c. dried cranberries
¹/₂ c. chopped dried apricots
¹/₂ c. dried currants
¹/₂ c. Sherry wine vinegar
2 T. walnut oil or olive oil
2 T. chopped fresh sage or 2
  tsp. dried rubbed sage
1 c. coarsely chopped pecans

Heat oil in large saucepan over medium-high heat. Add shallots and sauté until translucent, about 5 minutes. Add brown rice, wild rice, and wheat berries (available at natural food stores). Stir to coat. Add 2 c. water and 2 c. stock. Bring to boil. Reduce heat to low. Cover and cook until grains are tender and liquid is absorbed, about 40 minutes. Remove from heat. Stir cranberries, apricots, and currants into grain mixture. Cool to room temperature. Whisk vinegar, walnut oil, and sage in small bowl to blend. Pour over salad and toss to coat. Season generously with salt and pepper. Can be prepared one day ahead. Cover and refrigerate. Bring to room temperature before serving. Stir pecans into salad and serve. Serves eight.

Recipe Note: Susan Chambers taught at several Jackson area schools from 1957-1994, when she retired. Her former husband's family homesteaded on Mormon Row. Susan got this healthy recipe from Bon Appetit magazine some years ago.

"Be sure you put your feet in the right place, then stand firm."
- Abraham Lincoln

38140-01

Vegetables

STEWED TOMATOES

Lokey Lytjen
Jackson Hole resident since 1993

4 or 5 strips of bacon
about 1½ c. onion, diced
about 1 c. celery, diced
about ¾ c. bell pepper, diced

2 cans tomatoes, cut
pinch of sugar
salt
pepper

Fry bacon, and drain on paper towels. Reserve some of the bacon drippings. Sauté onion and celery in bacon drippings until transparent. Add tomatoes. Add salt and pepper to taste. Add sugar. Bring to a boil; then simmer on medium low heat about half an hour. You may need to simmer a bit longer at higher altitudes. Serve over cooked, long grain white rice; or serve them mixed together. Possible variations include adding a can of drained, whole kernel corn to make Corn Stewed Tomatoes; or adding fresh (or frozen) okra, sautéed, to make Okra and Tomatoes. Substitute turkey bacon and corn or canola oil for a healthier version, or add additional seasonings such as Tabasco, Lea and Perrins, and Parmesan cheese. These are especially good if you serve it with the cooked rice mixed together with the stewed tomatoes.

Recipe Note: Lokey moved here from Savannah, Georgia. Rice and tomatoes, or red rice as it is also called in the South, is one of Lokey's favorite foods. It complements ham, chicken, pork chops, and seafood. Lokey is Executive Director of the Jackson Hole Historical Society & Museum.

POTATO CROQUETTES

Genevieve Van Vleck
Member of the Pure Food Club

1 pt. mashed potatoes
1 T. butter
1 T. salt
¼ T. pepper

1 T. chopped parsley
¼ T. onion juice
one egg, separated

Boil and mash potatoes. Add seasonings. When done enough to handle, add yolk of egg. Roll into a ball and then into a cylinder. Roll in bread crumbs, then in white of egg, slightly beaten. Then roll in bread crumbs again. Fry in deep fat. Drain on brown paper.

Recipe Note: This recipe was included in a hand-written book Genevieve's mother wrote for her when she married Roy Van Vleck and moved to Jackson Hole. Genevieve's daughter, Jean Stewart, says this was a family favorite while she was growing up.

CHEESE GRITS

Debby Hodges
Jackson Hole resident since 1985

1 c. grits
2 c. milk
2 c. water
1 stick margarine or butter

dash of garlic powder
1 lb. Velveeta cheese, cubed
2 eggs, beaten well

Put grits in pan. Gradually stir in water and milk. Bring to a boil and simmer a few minutes until thick. Add margarine. Stir until melted. Add cheese, garlic, and well-beaten eggs. Stir until all egg whites have disappeared, cheese has melted, and mixture is smooth. Pour into a well-greased 1½ quart casserole dish. Bake at 350° for 40-50 minutes until it sets up. Serve hot.

Recipe Note: Debby grew up in Kentucky and has enjoyed this Southern dish ever since she found the recipe in a cookbook. While her husband Moe wouldn't eat grits at first, he loves Cheese Grits. This recipe has become a holiday staple at the Hodges house.

GARLIC MASHED SWEET POTATOES

Amy Manhart
Jackson Hole resident since 1995

2 lbs. fresh sweet potatoes or yams, quartered
2 cloves garlic, finely chopped
6 T. butter, divided

1 tsp. salt
½ c. sour cream
1 to 2 T. chopped cilantro

Cook unpeeled sweet potatoes, covered, in boiling salted water, 20-30 minutes or until tender. Meanwhile, sauté garlic in 1 Tablespoon butter for 2 minutes. When potatoes are fully cooked, drain thoroughly. Peel, dice, and return to pan. Add sautéed garlic, remaining butter, sour cream, and salt. Mash thoroughly. Fold in cilantro. Transfer to serving bowl and garnish with additional cilantro if desired. Makes 4 to 6 servings.

Recipe Note: Amy got this recipe off the Internet. For a lighter version, she uses only enough butter to sauté garlic and substitutes plain or vanilla yogurt for the sour cream. Amy came here to work for Grand Teton National Park. She now teaches in Teton County Schools and runs the GAP! program.

38140-01

SURPRISE POTATOES AU GRATIN

Jackie Richardson
Jackson Hole resident since 1972

2 lb. pkg. frozen hash brown
  potatoes
2 cans undiluted cream of
  mushroom, cream of chicken,
  or cream of potato soup

1 pt. sour cream
1 T. dried onion
1½ c. grated cheddar cheese
salt and/or pepper to taste

Defrost potatoes slightly. Combine all ingredients. Place into a 9 x 13-inch pan and bake at 325° for 1 hour and 15 minutes. Top with grated cheese and bake 15 more minutes.

Recipe Note: Jackie got this recipe from her husband Weldon's sister, Myrna Condie. It makes a delicious side dish.

MARINATED CARROTS

Debby Hodges
Jackson Hole resident since 1985

2 lbs. carrots, baby carrots work
  well
1 can tomato soup, undiluted
½ c. oil
½ c. sugar
1 tsp. salt

2 tsp. mustard
⅛ tsp. pepper
2 tsp. Worcestershire sauce
1 sm. chopped onion
1 chopped or sliced green
  pepper

Cook carrots until tender. Drain. Mix, but do not heat: tomato soup, oil, sugar, salt, mustard, pepper, and Worcestershire sauce. Pour over hot carrots. The longer this marinates, the better. Before serving, add onion and green pepper to the complete mixture. Serve either hot or cold.

Recipe Note: Debby and Moe Hodges have one daughter. Debby works at the Antler Motel, and Moe works at Jackson Hole Airport. Debby, who grew up in Kentucky, got this recipe from a friend's mother in Kentucky. It has become a family favorite.

"Minds are like parachutes - they only function when open."
- Thomas Dewar

RICE PILAF

Anna Ferrin
Jackson Hole native born in Kelly in 1908

1 small bunch of green onions
1 c. Minute Rice
a little butter
2 sm. cans button mushrooms

1 14-oz. can chicken broth
1 sm. can sliced water
  chestnuts

Chop onions fine, up into the green. Fry onions in butter for just a minute in a skillet, stirring often. Don't let them brown. Add broth, rice, mushrooms (including liquid), and water chestnuts (including liquid). Add any seasonings you like. Anna uses lemon pepper, salt, and garlic salt. Bring to a boil and boil a minute or two. Mix well, and pour in a 1½ quart casserole dish. Bake at 350° for 30-50 minutes. For variety, cooked meat and a cream soup could be added.

Recipe Note: Anna Ferrin, who just turned 93, is one of the oldest living Jackson Hole natives around. She has a wealth of information about the history of this valley. Anna worked in Ma Reed's restaurant in the 1920s. She got this delicious recipe from her cousin. It almost makes a meal by itself.

HASHED BROWN POTATOES

Genevieve Van Vleck
Member of the Pure Food Club

salt pork
2 c. cold boiled potatoes, finely
  chopped

⅛ T. pepper and salt if needed

Cut salt pork into small cubes, and fry out the fat. Then remove the scraps. Add cold boiled potatoes, and then salt and pepper. Mix potatoes thoroughly with the fat, and cook three minutes, stirring constantly. Let stand to brown underneath. Fold like an omelet, and serve on a hot platter.

Recipe Note: Genevieve's mother wrote this recipe in her cookbook for Genevieve to take to Wyoming when she married. "Mother was a clever cook, after she learned how," Jean Stewart says. "She'd look at a recipe and say, 'This looks a little odd,' so she'd dump something else in, and it was usually wonderful."

38140-01

Main Dishes & Casseroles

njoying a meal at an early Jackson Hole Hunting Camp

Collection of the Jackson Hole Historical Society & Museum

38140-ca-4

A tent dinner at the Moosehead Ranch

Collection of the Jackson Hole Historical Society & Museum

38140-ca-4b

Main Dishes

TURKEY ROLLS

Boyd Wilde
Jackson Hole resident since 1967

1¼ lb. diced cooked chicken or turkey
8 oz. pkg. softened cream cheese

lemon pepper to taste
1 can refrigerated crescent rolls
1 can cream of mushroom soup
½ soup can of milk

Mix together well: meat, cream cheese, and lemon pepper. Set aside. Spread out crescent rolls, and separate into triangles. To make larger rolls, dough can be rolled thinner with a floured rolling pin. Place a large spoonful of meat mixture in center of each roll. Wrap dough around meat mixture, sealing edges. Bake as directed on crescent roll package until rolls are lightly browned. Mix and heat mushroom soup with ½ can of milk to make a gravy. Baked rolls can be frozen and reheated later.

Recipe Note: Boyd and Fern Wilde raised seven children, two of whom still live in Jackson Hole. Boyd is Breakfast Manager at the Teton Steakhouse. He doesn't remember who gave him this recipe, but it's a simple, easy way to dress up leftover turkey or chicken.

"We can do no great things, only small things with great love."
- Mother Teresa

PIZZA SAUCE AND DOUGH

Chrystal Nethercott
Jackson Hole native

Sauce:

2 T. olive oil	1 c. mild onion, chopped
1 c. tomato sauce	1 tsp. Italian herbs
1/8 tsp. garlic powder	

Dough:

1 1/2 c. warm water	1 tsp. salt
1 T. yeast	3-4 c. flour
1 T. sugar	

For sauce, brown onion in oil on medium low heat for 20 minutes. Add all other sauce ingredients. Simmer and stir 15 minutes. Sauce may be made ahead and frozen, or kept in refrigerator up to a week. Makes 1 1/8 cups. For dough, stir yeast into warm water and let sit 5-10 minutes. Mix in sugar, salt, and flour. Knead 5 minutes. Let rise 30-45 minutes. Roll out, place in pans, and cover with cooled sauce. Add favorite toppings and cheese. Bake at 400° for 15-20 minutes.

Recipe Note: Chrystal Nethercott got this recipe from a brick kit for making pizza. She has used it to feed her family and other groups. Chrystal is an excellent cook, and her pizzas and other recipes have become legendary in the valley. Her husband Bob is also a Jackson Hole native.

CALICO BEANS

Donna Goutermont
Jackson Hole resident since 1984

1 lb. hamburger	1 tsp. mustard
1/2 lb. bacon	1/2 c. catsup
2 tsp. vinegar	1 can pork and beans
1 tsp. salt	1 can kidney beans
3/4 c. brown sugar	1 can butter beans
1 medium onion, chopped	1 can lima beans

Brown bacon. Remove from pan. Pour off grease. In same pan, brown hamburger and onion. Drain. Mix in all other ingredients. Pour into a casserole dish, and bake at 350° for 40 minutes.

Recipe Note: Donna got this recipe from her husband Galen's mother, who lives in Montana. This recipe is sometimes called Roosevelt Beans because Teddy Roosevelt reportedly loved it and requested it every time he stayed at the OTO Ranch outside of Gardiner, Montana.

38140-01

DUTCH OVEN CHICKEN DINNER

Joyce Rudd
Jackson Hole resident since 1968

4 lg. boneless chicken breasts
1 to 1½ c. potatoes, cubed
1 to 1½ c. zucchini, cubed
1 to 1½ c. carrots, cubed
1 to 1½ c. cabbage, chopped
1 can Garbanzo beans with juice

1 med. chopped onion
¼ c. chopped green pepper
2-3 chopped garlic cloves
1 med. can chicken broth
1 can cream of chicken soup
salt and pepper

On outdoor barbeque, grill chicken breasts until brown on both sides. Place cut up potatoes, zucchini, carrots, and cabbage in bottom of a 12-inch Dutch Oven. Mix in Garbanzo beans with juice, onion, green pepper, and garlic cloves. Place chicken breasts over top of vegetables. Pour chicken broth over meat and vegetables. Spoon out and spread cream of chicken soup over top of chicken. Season with salt and pepper as desired. Cover and cook on low to medium heat on outdoor grill for 1 to 1½ hours until vegetables are tender.

Recipe Note: This recipe was a favorite of the crew and wranglers at Teton Trail Rides when the Rudds operated the concession in Grand Teton National Park from 1950 to 1993. This makes a hearty outdoor meal.

TACO PIE

Marlene Cox
Jackson Hole resident since 1993

1 lb. ground beef or 1 pkg. tofu
1 pkg. taco or chili seasoning
1 14-oz. can tomato sauce or
  salsa
1 16-oz. container sour cream
1 8-oz. pkg. shredded cheddar
  cheese (or cheddar/jack
  cheese mix)

1 can (refrigerated type)
  crescent rolls, about 8 rolls
1 14-oz. pkg. Doritos, Nacho
  Cheese flavor, crushed

Fry ground beef, draining fat. If using tofu, mix with salsa and fry. Add seasoning and tomato sauce or salsa. In a large pie pan coated with cooking oil spray, spread out crescent rolls, and press to make a seamless crust. Sprinkle half of crushed Doritos on crust. Pour meat or tofu mixture over chips. Spread sour cream on meat. Then sprinkle with the rest of the Doritos. Cover with shredded cheese. Bake uncovered 20-30 minutes in 350° oven or until crust is golden brown and cheese is lightly toasted.

Recipe Note: Marlene Cox is a Wyoming native. She and her daughter Jenny enjoy hiking in Grand Teton National Park. Marlene got this delicious main dish recipe from her sister years ago.

29

SHIPWRECK

Chris Miller
Jackson Hole native

2 med. potatoes, cut into small
  cubes
1 can tomato soup
1 med. onion, diced
1 med. can pork and beans

salt and pepper to taste
1 lb. ground beef, browned and
  drained
$\frac{1}{4}$ c. water

Mix all ingredients together in an ungreased 1½ quart casserole dish. Bake uncovered 1 hour at 350° or until potatoes are tender.

Recipe Note: Chris Miller, the daughter of Man and Vi McCain, got this recipe from her Aunt Ella Mercill, Man McCain's sister. Chris has often doubled this recipe to feed the Teton Boating crew at Jenny Lake. Chris' parents and grandparents were influential in the settling and development of Jackson Hole.

APPLES AND BUTTONS
(Schnitz un Knepp)

Happy Chambers Weston
Jackson Hole resident since she was 5 years old

1 pt. dried apples
1 lb. smoked ham
1 T. brown sugar
1 c. flour
2 tsp. baking powder

1 tsp. salt
pepper to taste
1 egg, well beaten
½ c. milk

Cover dried apples with water and soak overnight. In the morning, cover ham with water and simmer 2 hours. Add apples and soaking water and simmer about 1 more hour. Add brown sugar. For Dumplings: Sift together flour, baking powder, salt and pepper. Mix together milk, egg, and stir into flour quickly until just mixed. Drop by tablespoons into simmering ham and apples. Tightly cover kettle, and cook for 20 more minutes. Serve piping hot on a platter.

Recipe Note: Happy Weston got this old pioneer recipe from a friend's cookbook. It reflects Swiss and German influence on pioneer cooking.

38140-01

BEEF PIE

Charlene Bressler
Jackson Hole native

1 c. diced cooked roast beef	4 T. flour
1 c. diced cooked potatoes	¼ c. diced celery
¼ c. diced cooked carrots	1 tsp. salt
2 T. chopped onion	3 T. butter
¼ tsp. pepper	2 c. milk

Melt butter and add flour. Blend well and add milk. Cook until a creamy sauce forms. Add the rest of the ingredients and pour into a shallow, well buttered baking pan. Cover with dough.

Dough:

1½ c. flour	1 tsp. baking powder
¼ tsp. salt	3 T. fat
1 egg	½ c. milk

Mix flour, baking powder, and salt. Cut in the fat with a knife, and mixing with the knife, add the egg and milk. Spread over the meat mixture. Make four holes in the top to permit steam to escape. Bake in a moderate oven (350°) for 25 minutes. Serve in the dish in which it was baked.

Recipe Note: Charlene shared this old standby from her collection of old recipe clippings.

"The past is but the beginning of a beginning."

- H.G. Wells

PIEROGIES

Ski and Ruth Wynosky
Jackson Hole summer volunteers

1 egg	cheese
1 c. milk	chopped or sliced onions
1 tsp. salt	butter
hot mashed potatoes	

Blend egg, milk, and salt. Add enough flour to make a dough that can be rolled out. Roll out to ⅛ inch thick, and cut into 4-to 5-inch squares. Meanwhile, add however much you want of your favorite cheese to mashed potatoes. The Wynoskys use Velveeta, cut in cubes. If using a harder cheese, grate it. Blend cheese into potatoes until melted and mixed. Place a dollop of potato mixture in the center of each dough square. Fold dough over to form a triangle and crimp edges. Deep fry until golden brown. Sauté onions in butter until tender. Ladle over fried pierogies and eat. For variation, mix cooked hamburger with potatoes; or substitute shredded, cooked, seasoned cabbage or Black Angus dry cottage cheese as filling.

Recipe Note: Leonard "Ski" and Ruth Wynosky, from California, have worked several summers for the Bridger-Teton National Forest. They have volunteered for 13 years, working for various government agencies. This recipe is a family favorite from Ski's Polish heritage. It's rich and delicious.

"For after all, the best thing one can do when it's raining is to let it rain."
- Henry Wadsworth Longfellow

38140-01

Casseroles

CHICKEN IN A POT(HOLE) CASSEROLE

Carol Richardson
Jackson Hole resident more than 20 years

1 large roasting chicken, baked
1 c. diced celery
2 cans cream of chicken soup
1 c. mayonnaise
2 T. sage
2 T. chicken flavored bouillon
  crystals

salt and pepper to taste
milk as needed to moisten
1 pkg. frozen broccoli, thawed
1 T. lemon juice (optional)
1 c. diced onion
2 c. cooked rice

Remove and discard skin from baked chicken. Cut meat into bite-sized pieces. Mix all ingredients together, and place in 9 x 13-inch casserole dish. Top with approximately 4 c. store-bought dressing cubes. Pat down slightly. Bake in 350° oven for 45 minutes or till hot. Add more rice if mixture is too wet, more milk if too dry.

Recipe Note: Carol Richardson and husband Hal have four children. Carol served as a member of the Jackson Town Council beginning in 1997. Her campaign slogan was "a chicken in every pothole." An active member of the GOP, Carol is also a writer and watercolorist.

GREEN CHILI FRITATTA

Marge Ryan
Jackson Hole Native born on Mormon Row

4 cans whole green chilies
2 lbs. grated jack cheese
2 lbs. grated cheddar cheese
1 dozen eggs

9 T. flour
4 c. canned milk
green chili salsa

Remove seeds from green chilies, and lay flat in bottom of large baking pan. Sprinkle grated cheeses on top of chilies. Beat eggs with flour and canned milk. Pour mixture over chilies and cheese. Bake 1 hour at 350° (or until set). Remove from oven and brush with green chili salsa. Return to oven for 10 minutes. Remove, and let set 10 minutes before cutting and serving.

Recipe Note: Marge Ryan, one of Jackson's fine cooks, recently retired from her position as the Teton County Elections Clerk. Marge got this recipe from Edna Jones, former Teton County Assessor. It's a popular potluck recipe.

PORK CHOP CASSEROLE

Laraine McCollum
Jackson Hole resident since 1965

1 pkg. frozen hash browns
1 tsp. salt
6 boneless pork chops, 1/2-3/4 inches thick
2 T. oil
1 can cream of mushroom soup, undiluted

1 2/3 c. chicken broth
1 can (2.8 oz.) dried French-fried onions
3/4 c. flour
1/2 tsp. pepper
8 oz. sour cream

Spread hash browns in bottom of 9 x 13-inch ungreased pan. Salt and pepper well. Combine flour with 1 teaspoon salt and 1/2 teaspoon pepper, and dredge pork chops in this mixture. Heat oil in fry pan. Cook chops approximately 6 minutes per side or until they are well browned. Place chops in a single layer over hash browns in baking pan. In a separate bowl, combine soup, 1 cup chicken broth, and sour cream. Mix well. Pour over chops. Sprinkle with French-fried onions. Pour remaining 2/3 cup of chicken broth around edges of pan into the potatoes. Cover pan with foil and bake at 350° one hour and 15 minutes or until chops are done.

Recipe Note: Laraine McCollum combined three other recipes to create this one several years ago. It has been a hit at family get-togethers. Laraine has published several cookbooks. She and husband Ed have three children.

HUNGRY WRANGLERS' CASSEROLE

Joyce Rudd
Jackson Hole resident since 1968

2 lg. potatoes, sliced
1 med. onion, chopped
1 lb. hamburger, browned and drained
1 minced garlic clove (opt.)
chopped green pepper (opt.)

sliced mushrooms (opt.)
1 large can (1 lb. 14 oz.) pork and beans
1 can tomato soup mixed with 1 can water

Layer potatoes, onion, hamburger, garlic, green pepper, and onion in large, greased casserole dish. Spread pork and beans over this layer. Then top with mixture of tomato soup and water. Bake uncovered 1 hour at 375° or until done.

Recipe Note: The Rudd family operated Teton Trail Rides in Grand Teton National Park from 1950 to 1993. Joyce used this hearty, low-cost recipe to feed their crew.

38140-01

STUFFED GREEN PEPPERS

Laraine McCollum
Jackson Hole resident since 1965

4 large green peppers
1 lb. hamburger
1/2 c. fine Italian bread crumbs
1 onion, chopped fine
1/2 tsp. salt

1/8 tsp. pepper
1/2 tsp. basil
1 1/2 c. cooked rice
1 1/2 c. tomato sauce
1 c. shredded cheese

Wash peppers. Cut in half lengthwise. Remove seeds and membrane. Brown hamburger, onion, salt, and pepper. Then sprinkle on basil. Stir in rice, 3/4 cup tomato sauce, 1/2 c. cheese, and bread crumbs. Fill green pepper halves with mixture. Place in microproof baking dish. Top each with remaining tomato sauce. Cover with waxed paper, and cook on high for 16-18 minutes until peppers are tender. Uncover; sprinkle on remaining cheese. Microwave for 1 or 2 minutes, until cheese melts.

Recipe Note: Laraine and Ed McCollum have three grown children. This recipe was originally published in one of Laraine's own cookbooks.

TACO MEAT CASSEROLE

Mike Gates
Jackson Hole resident since 1989

1 lb. ground beef
1 pkg. taco seasoning
2 14-oz. cans tomato sauce

1 12-oz. pkg. corkscrew noodles
1 15-oz. can corn, drained
grated cheddar cheese

Brown ground beef. Drain and add taco seasoning. Boil noodles until tender. Mix together meat, noodles, corn, and tomato sauce. Bake uncovered in large casserole dish at 350° for 40 minutes. Sprinkle with enough grated cheese to cover top of casserole, and return to oven until cheese is melted.

Recipe Note: Mike Gates met and married his wife Brandy in 1991. They have three children. Mike got this recipe from his mother. This easy, low-cost, delicious main dish makes enough to feed four hungry adults. Mike works at Albertson's.

STUFFED JUMBO SHELLS

Ron Veitel
Moved to Jackson Hole in 1997

3 c. tomato sauce
4 oz. jumbo macaroni shells,
  cooked
1½ lbs. mashed tofu OR 1 lb.
  mashed tofu and ½ lb. grated
  Mozzarella cheese

¼ c. chopped fresh parsley
1½ tsp. salt or sea salt
½ tsp. basil
2 T. onion powder
½ tsp. garlic powder

Have ready: tomato sauce and cooked macaroni shells. Combine tofu, mozzarella, parsley, salt, basil, onion powder, and garlic powder. Spread 2 c. tomato sauce on bottom of a 9 x 9-inch pan. Spoon tofu mixture into cooked pasta shells, about ⅓ cup per shell, and arrange in pan. Add ½ c. water to remaining tomato sauce. Then pour stripes of sauce over top of the stuffed shells. Bake at 350° until sauce is bubbly, about 25 minutes.

Recipe Note: Ron Veitel has worked in several food service jobs in Jackson Hole. He has been a vegetarian for many years and loves to cook for others. This recipe always wins a seal of approval. Even if you're not a vegetarian, it's a great main dish.

CHICKEN ENCHILADA CASSEROLE

Lynne Marie Palmer
Jackson Hole resident since 1983

1 10-¾ oz. can of cream of
  chicken soup
1 soup can of milk
1 med. onion, chopped
1 4-oz. can diced green chilies,
  drained

1 to 2 c. cooked chicken chunks
  (may use canned)
10-12 corn tortillas, torn into
  pieces
½-1 c. grated cheese

Combine soup and milk. Stir in onion, chilies, chicken, and tortillas. Mix well. Pour into 1½ quart greased casserole dish. Cover and bake at 350° for 30 minutes. Part of cheese can be mixed in before baking, or just placed on top for the last few minutes of baking time, long enough to melt the cheese.

Recipe Note: Lynne Marie Palmer and husband Richard have three children. Richard is a CPA and partner at Thompson, Palmer, and Associates. This easy recipe is great for potluck dinners. Using skim milk and less cheese can make it relatively low fat. Or add other ingredients, such as chopped olives.

38140-01

TATER TOT CASSEROLE

Mike Gates
Jackson Hole resident since 1989

1 lb. ground beef
½ diced onion
1 family sized can of either
 cream of mushroom or cream
 of chicken soup

1 regular-sized can of either
 cream of mushroom or cream
 of chicken soup
32-oz. pkg. frozen tater tots
grated cheddar cheese

Brown ground beef with onion. Drain. Pour one family-sized can of soup and one regular-sized can of soup into a large bowl. If you use the large size of cream of mushroom, use the smaller size of cream of chicken, or vice versa. Mix; then add frozen tater tots and beef mixture. Stir well, and pour into a large greased casserole dish. Bake uncovered at 350° for 40 minutes, stirring mid-way through cooking. Sprinkle with grated cheddar cheese. Return to oven just long enough to melt cheese, and, as Mike says, "you're ready to rock."

Recipe Note: Mike got this recipe from his mother. It makes a scrumptious, easy main dish, great for having friends over. Mike works at Albertson's.

WESTERN HOSPITALITY CASSEROLE

Marge Ryan
Jackson Hole native born on Mormon Row

½ lb. of white beans
cold water
1 lb. hamburger
½ onion, chopped

1 12-oz. can tomato sauce
1½ c. cooked, sliced carrots
½ c. brown sugar
2 strips bacon

Soak beans in cold water overnight. Then cook until tender. Drain beans, reserving ¾ cup of liquid. Brown hamburger and onion. Drain off fat. Mix bean liquid with tomato sauce. Place half the beans in a large greased (Marge sprays it with Pam) casserole dish (at least 2-quart size). Cover beans with carrots and hamburger mixture. Then cover with the remaining beans. Pour tomato sauce mixture over the top. Sprinkle with brown sugar, and lay 2 strips of bacon on top. Bake uncovered at 350° for 30-45 minutes.

Recipe Note: Marge attended the Grovont School in the mid-1940s. Occasionally, her mother, Fay May, brought this dish to school. Although there was no "hot lunch" program, sometimes mothers of the 10-12 students there brought in a hot dish for everyone. This casserole became a Mormon Row favorite.

TURKEY BROCCOLI CASSEROLE

Carol McCain
Jackson Hole resident since 1976

1 pkg. frozen chopped broccoli
cooked leftover turkey slices
1 can cream of chicken soup
½ c. mayonnaise

1 T. lemon juice
½ tsp. curry powder
buttered bread crumbs

Thaw broccoli and spread in buttered casserole dish. Top broccoli with enough sliced turkey to cover it. Cover broccoli and turkey with sauce made by mixing the following together: cream of chicken soup, mayonnaise, lemon juice, and curry powder. Top with buttered bread crumbs. Bake at 350° for 30 minutes.

Recipe Note: Carol got this recipe when she lived in California. It was served at a church Christmas dinner and has become a favorite of two of Carol's three grown children. It's a great way to use leftover holiday turkey. Carol's late husband Art was the son of Man and Vi McCain.

Recipe Favorites

38140-01

Meat, Poultry, Fish & Wild Game

**Ben Goe, Ed Lumbeck, and Glenn Ferrin
show off a good catch of fish**

Collection of the Jackson Hole Historical Society & Museum

**Charles Fessler and Roger Slusser
hunting at Moran**

Collection of the Jackson Hole Historical Society & Museum

38140-ca-5b

Meat, Poultry, Fish & Wild Game

Meat

PAN BROILED STEAK

Genevieve Van Vleck
Member of the Pure Food Club

1-inch thick steaks
salt

pepper
butter

Have pan perfectly smooth and clean, and use no fat of any kind. When the smoke rises from the center of the pan, put in the meat. Cook for 1 minute on one side. Then turn with a broad-bladed knife and cook on the other side. When done, remove to a hot platter and add salt, pepper and a little butter. Steaks will require 4-6 minutes; lamb chops, 8-10 minutes; and chickens, 20 minutes.

Recipe Note: Genevieve Van Vleck's mother hand-wrote these pan broiling instructions for meats in a little book for Genevieve to take with her to Jackson Hole when she married Roy Van Vleck in 1911.

BBQ BRISKET

Nancy Effinger
Jackson Hole resident from 1972 until the 1990s

5-6 lb. brisket
3 oz. liquid smoke
celery salt
onion salt
garlic salt

salt & pepper
Worcestershire sauce
6 oz. BBQ sauce (not Hickory
 flavor)

Place brisket in a deep pan. Pour liquid smoke over it. Sprinkle with celery, onion, and garlic salt to taste. Cover and refrigerate overnight. The following day, sprinkle salt, pepper, and Worcestershire sauce to taste over brisket. Cover and bake five hours at 275°. Then uncover and pour BBQ sauce over meat. Return to oven uncovered and bake one hour longer. Remove from oven and cool at least one hour before serving.

Recipe Note: Nancy Effinger was director of Teton County Library for many years before moving from Jackson. She got this recipe from a friend.

BARBECUED RIBS

Eva Topping
Former owner of Moose Head Ranch

1½ c. catsup
1½ T. brown sugar
1 scant T. prepared mustard
1 scant T. red pepper (probably
  cayenne)

3 T. Worcestershire sauce
salt and pepper to taste

Mix and heat together in saucepan: catsup, brown sugar, red pepper, mustard, Worcestershire sauce, salt, and pepper. Pour over wild game or beef ribs, and bake 2 hours in a slow oven, about 325°. Serve with baked potatoes.

Recipe Note: Eva and Fred Topping owned and operated the Moose Head Ranch about 40 years. Eva did much of the cooking. This recipe, written in Eva's own handwriting, was contributed by her niece, Charlene Bressler.

VEGETABLE MEATBALLS

Carolyn Mellor
Jackson Hole native

2 lbs. ground beef
4 med. carrots, peeled & grated
4 med. potatoes, peeled &
  grated
½ c. chopped onion

2 eggs
1 c. bread crumbs
3 cans Cream of Celery soup
1½ soup cans of milk
pepper to taste

Mix ground beef with carrots, potatoes, onion, eggs, pepper, and bread crumbs. Shape into balls. Brown in skillet or under broiler. Place meatballs in a single layer in baking pan. Blend soup with milk, and pour over meatballs. Bake at 350° for 45 minutes.

Recipe Note: Carolyn got this recipe from her mother, Lillian Robertson. The Mellors' older children beg Carolyn to make this dish when they come home to visit. Carolyn is active in many community activities and is a superb cook.

"Food: Part of the spiritual expression of the French, and I do not believe that they have ever heard of calories."

- Beverly Baxter

TETON CHICKEN

Karen Fox
Lived in Jackson in 1990s

4 chicken breasts
1/4 c. Teton mustard
1/4 c. Yellowstone salad
  dressing

2 T. dry onion soup mix
1 clove minced garlic
2 T. peach jam
pepper to taste

Brown chicken in fry pan with a small amount of oil. Set chicken aside. In fry pan, brown garlic. Then add Teton mustard, peach jam, Yellowstone dressing, and dry onion soup mix. Cook, stirring until well blended and hot. Arrange chicken in baking dish and cover with sauce. Pepper to taste. Bake at 350° until done (30 minutes or until meat is no longer pink in center).

Recipe Note: Karen Fox lived in Jackson in the late 1990s before moving to Utah.

SMOKED HOLIDAY TURKEY

Marilyn Nelson
Jackson Hole resident since 1988

1 12-lb. turkey
1 3½-oz. bottle of Liquid Smoke
2 c. Tender Quick tenderizer

1 c. canning salt
salad oil

Mix Tender Quick, Liquid Smoke, and salt with enough water to completely cover turkey in a glass or plastic container. Soak for 24 hours. Drain, rinse, and dry turkey. Oil skin of turkey with salad oil, and bake uncovered for 1 hour at 350°, then for about another 10 hours at 250°. Serve with other holiday fixin's.

Recipe Note: Marilyn got this recipe from her mother-in-law. It's a delicious alternative to the traditional roasted holiday bird. Marilyn works at Knobe's Office Supply. She and husband Brett have two children.

CHICKEN LINDA

Linda Drumm
Moved to Jackson Hole in 1997

3 boneless chicken breasts, cut
  into strips
4 T. butter
1 tsp. crushed garlic

1 c. sour cream
1 can cream of mushroom soup
salt and pepper to taste

Heat butter in large frying pan; sauté chicken with garlic. Cook until chicken is done. Over low heat, stir in sour cream and cream of mushroom soup. (Optional: Mix in ½ cup white wine with sour cream and soup.) Add salt and pepper. Simmer until hot. Serve over rice or egg noodles. Serves six.

Recipe Note: Linda created this simple, easy recipe herself. Her family loves it. Linda and husband Michael have moved from the valley.

Fish

CREAM OF CABBAGE SOUP WITH FISH

Daisy Tucker
Jackson Hole native

1 head of green cabbage
1 onion, mild or strong,
  according to your taste
3 oz. smoked trout or salmon
1½ qt. chicken stock

1 T. fresh thyme or 1 pinch
  dried thyme
3 c. heavy cream
salt and pepper

Cut cabbage into 1-inch pieces. Finely dice bacon. Mince onion. Cut fish into shreds. Heat up chicken stock. Cook bacon in a large, heavy stock pot until almost crisp, about 4 minutes. Add onion, and cook over medium heat until tender, about 5 minutes. Add cabbage and dried thyme, if using dried. Cook until cabbage is soft, about 5 minutes. Add hot chicken stock, and bring to a boil. Reduce heat to a simmer, and cook about 20 minutes. Add cream, and return soup to a boil. Add fresh thyme, if using fresh, and season to taste with salt and pepper. Pour into warm soup bowls, and garnish with shredded fish.

Recipe Note: Daisy Tucker, daughter of Bennie and Kitty Linn, married Jesse Tucker. Both were schoolteachers in Jackson Hole for many years. Daisy got this recipe from a computer cookbook, but maintains she used this basic recipe for years before computers. Unsmoked fish can be used.

38140-01

CRAB CAKES

Erma Nethercott
Jackson Hole native, born and raised on the Elk Refuge

1 lb. fresh mushrooms, sliced
3 eggs
1/4 c. minced onion
1 c. soft bread crumbs

1 c. crab meat
4 1/2 T. mayonnaise
3 tsp. lemon juice

Lay mushrooms in greased 9 x 13-inch cake pan. Mix together crab meat, eggs, mayonnaise, onion, and lemon juice. Pour over mushrooms. Top with bread crumbs. Bake at 375° for 30 minutes. Remove and cut into squares before serving.

Recipe Note: Erma Nethercott's parents were homesteaders James and Berla Chambers. Erma was their third child. She married Moy Nethercott, and they had three children. One son still lives in Jackson. Erma currently resides at St. John's Living Center. This delicious recipe was always a favorite for company.

SHRIMP PASTA SALAD

Sharon Nethercott
Jackson Hole native

1 16-oz. pkg. Penne pasta, cooked and rinsed in cold water
1 lb. cooked shelled shrimp
1 sm. can diced green chilies
1 sm. can sliced black olives, drained
1 c. diced celery (or about 2 T. celery seed, to taste)

1 c. diced red onion
1-2 c. mayonnaise (more is better)
coarse ground black pepper to taste
2 T. McCormick Salad Supreme seasoning (or to taste)

Mix together pasta, shrimp, chilies, olives, celery, onion, mayonnaise, and seasonings. Taste, and add salt if needed. Chill before serving. This salad is best if it sits overnight in the refrigerator.

Recipe Note: After being born in Jackson, Sharon Nethercott was raised on the Dockham Ranch in Bondurant. She moved back here and married Neal Nethercott. Sharon admits she stole parts of this recipe from her mother-in-law, Erma Nethercott, an exceptional cook.

ETOUFEE (SHRIMP OR CRAYFISH)

Cindy Butler
Jackson Hole resident since 1996

2½ lbs. seafood (cleaned)
½ lb. margarine
1 lg. onion, chopped
1 bell pepper, chopped
5 T. cornstarch
1½ T. paprika

5 T. green onions, chopped
5 c. water
½ tsp. salt
1 tsp. cayenne pepper
¼ stalk of celery, chopped

In large stock pot, melt margarine. Season seafood with salt and cayenne pepper. Add paprika to margarine. Add onions, pepper, and celery. Sauté 10 minutes. Add seafood to pot, along with 5 cups water. Stir and simmer 20 minutes. Check for taste, and add garlic powder and black pepper to taste. Make thickening mixture with cornstarch and small amount of water. Add thickening to pot until seafood mixture is slightly thick. Serve over hot, cooked rice. Sprinkle with chopped green onions. Serves 12.

Recipe Note: Cindy Butler used to live in New Orleans. She begged a chef to teach her how to make this delicious spicy cajun dish. This recipe makes a large batch. Cindy enjoys serving this dish at dinner parties. She works at Blue Spruce Cleaners.

ORANGE ROUGHY PARMESAN

Joyce Sawczuk
Jackson Hole Resident since 1993

orange roughy fillets
2 T. mayonnaise
2 T. Parmesan cheese, grated

dash Worcestershire sauce
1 tsp. lemon juice
Progresso bread crumbs

Mix well: mayonnaise, Parmesan, Worcestershire sauce, and lemon juice, making it into a paste. Spread a thin layer of paste over fillets in a baking pan. Sprinkle crumbs over cheese mixture. Bake at 425° for 15 minutes.

Recipe Note: Joyce is Office Manager at the Jackson Hole Historical Society and Museum. She enjoys preparing meals for family and friends. This fast and easy main dish can be made with ingredients most people already have at home.

38140-01

TUNA WALNUT FETTUCCINE

Joyce Sawczuk
Jackson Hole resident since 1993

12-oz. pkg. fettuccine egg
  noodles
10-oz. pkg. frozen peas
2 6-oz. cans tuna, drained and
  flaked, reserve oil
1 T. olive oil

1 c. walnuts, chopped
1 c. ricotta cheese
1/2 c. grated Romano cheese,
  plus more for topping
1 tsp. Tabasco
1/2 tsp. salt

Prepare fettuccine noodles per package directions. During last 2 minutes of cooking noodles, stir in frozen peas. Drain fettuccine and peas. Meanwhile, in large bowl, combine flaked tuna, tuna oil, olive oil, walnuts, ricotta cheese, Romano cheese, Tabasco, and salt. Add cooked fettuccine and peas to mixture; toss to mix well. Sprinkle with extra Romano cheese if desired. Makes 6 servings.

Recipe Note: Joyce is Office Manager at the Jackson Hole Historical Society & Museum. She got this recipe from a magazine. This fancy tuna noodle casserole is a hit with friends and family.

Wild Game

STROGANOFF

Marge Ryan
Jackson Hole native born on Mormon Row

2 lbs. elk steak
1/2 c. butter or margarine
1 can sliced mushrooms
1/2 c. chopped onion

2 cans bouillon soup
5 T. flour
salt and pepper to taste
rice or noodles

Cut steak into strips approximately 1/4-inch thick and 1/4-inch wide. Brown quickly in a skillet in butter. Push meat to one side, and add sliced mushrooms and onion. Cook till tender, but not brown. Add two cans bouillon soup. Heat just to boiling. Blend soup with flour. Stir into broth. Cook, stirring constantly till thickened. Add salt and pepper to taste, and serve over hot cooked rice or noodles. Serves 5 or 6.

Recipe Note: While this recipe can be used equally as well for beef, it is an excellent way to prepare elk. When Marge's children were young, the family ate elk meat a lot. This recipe was an old standby. "It was really good," Marge says.

WILD GAME CASSEROLE

Jean Van Vleck Stewart
Jackson Hole resident since 1920

**2 lbs. or more wild game stew
  meat**
at least 3 slices of bread

**flour seasoned with salt,
  pepper, and garlic salt**
bacon grease and butter

Roll bite-sized pieces of meat in seasoned flour. Brown meat in bacon grease with a little bit of butter. Eat as you go along, if desired. When meat is browned, remove from pan, add more bacon grease and butter. Cut bread lengthwise into strips about ¾ inches wide. Brown in bacon grease and butter. Place in bottom of a casserole dish. Stack into layers if necessary. Place browned meat on top. Melt 1 beef bouillon cube in 1 c. water, or use 1 can beef broth. Pour over meat and bread strips. Bake in oven at 350° for 1 hour to 1 hour and 15 minutes or until moisture is absorbed.

Recipe Note: Jean Van Vleck Stewart got this recipe from a friend during World War II. It's a simple way to make wild game tasty. Beef or other meats can also be substituted. This recipe has become a family favorite.

Recipe Favorites

38140-01

Pies, Pastry & Desserts

Picnicking

Collection of the Jackson Hole Historical Society & Museum

38140-ca-6

Kay's Bluebird Cafe, 1939

Collection of the Jackson Hole Historical Society & Museum

38140-ca-6b

Pies, Pastry & Desserts

Pies

LEMON PIE FILLING

Alta Webb
Jackson Hole resident for many years

2 c. water
¾ c. sugar
½ tsp. salt
5 or 6 T. lemon juice

2 egg yolks
2 T. cornstarch
lump of butter if desired

In saucepan, mix together water, sugar, salt, egg yolks, and cornstarch. Heat to boiling, stirring constantly. When mixture is thick, stir in lemon juice and butter. Cook a minute or two. Remove from heat. Cool a few minutes, and pour into a cooked pie shell. Top with meringue.

Recipe Note: Alta Webb, Clarene Law's mother, was an excellent cook. "Mom was famous for her lemon pies," Clarene says. "She was the best." Alta and her husband lived in tents while he helped build the first travelable road over Sylvan Pass in Yellowstone Park.

RHUBARB MERINGUE PIE

Leora Robertson
Jackson Hole resident since 1932

3 c. rhubarb, cleaned and cut
  into 1-inch pieces
1 to 2 c. sugar, to taste
3 T. flour

2 eggs (whole or yolks only if
  you make meringue)
pinch of salt
unbaked, 9-inch pie shell

Combine sugar and flour. Beat in eggs and salt. Add rhubarb. Pour mixture into pie shell. Cover with either a top crust or lattice crust, and bake at 450° for 30 minutes. Or try Leora's favorite topping, meringue.

Meringue:

2 egg whites at room
  temperature

4 T. sugar

Use only yolks in pie. While pie is baking, beat egg whites until they stand up in peaks. Mix in sugar slowly. After pie has baked, cover with meringue and bake at 450° about 5 minutes longer or until meringue is golden brown.

BEST COCONUT CREAM PIE

Carol Cavaner
Moved to Jackson Hole in 1997

½ c. sugar
3 T. cornstarch
1 c. canned evaporated milk
¼ tsp. salt
3 beaten egg yolks
1½ c. milk
1 c. flaked coconut
2 tsp. vanilla

1 tsp. coconut flavoring
2 T. butter
3 egg whites
½ tsp. baking powder
2 T. sugar
1 tsp. vanilla
½ c.+ flaked coconut

Stir together well with a wire whisk: sugar, cornstarch, evaporated milk, salt, egg yolks, and milk. Continue to stir mixture constantly over medium heat until it comes to a boil. Boil 2 minutes. Then add 1 cup flaked coconut, vanilla, coconut flavoring and butter. Stir well. Pour into 9-inch baked pie shell. While pie is cooling, beat egg whites. Add baking powder, 2 Tablespoons sugar, and 1 teaspoon vanilla while continuing to beat until stiff peaks form. Then fold in ½ cup coconut with a spatula. Spread mixture over pie. Sprinkle with coconut. Bake at 350° until lightly browned, 10-15 minutes. Cool and enjoy.

Recipe Note: Carol Cavaner has worked in various shops in Jackson Hole. She enjoys creating recipes and giving samples away. This pie makes a great holiday or otherwise dessert.

FROZEN PUMPKIN PIE

Laraine McCollum
Jackson Hole resident since 1965

½ lb. marshmallows
1 can pumpkin (3½ c.)
1 tsp. cinnamon

¼ tsp. ginger
¼ tsp. salt
1 c. whipping cream

Heat and stir marshmallows, ginger, pumpkin, cinnamon, and salt until melted and mixed. Cool 1 hour. Whip cream, and stir into pumpkin mixture. Pour into baked pie shell. Freeze uncovered. Wrap and store in freezer. Before serving, thaw for 40 minutes at room temperature. Unwrap and serve.

Recipe Note: Laraine doesn't remember where she got this recipe. It makes a delicious dessert that can be made from leftover pumpkin from Halloween and frozen ahead for Thanksgiving.

38140-01

MY GRANDMA'S CHOCOLATE PIE

Jill (McClelland) Russell
Jackson Hole resident since 1997

3 eggs, separated
1 c. sugar
½ c. flour (good flour)
½ c. cocoa
1 can Carnation evaporated milk

1 c. boiling water
⅛ lb. butter
1 tsp. vanilla
pinch salt

Beat egg yolks. Add ½ cup sugar. Cream together. Then add 2 Table-spoons Carnation milk. Mix. Add balance of sugar, milk, ⅔ cup boiling water, and flour to yolks. Mix cocoa to a paste in ⅓ cup boiling water. Add salt to paste; then stir into creamed mixture. Cook until thick and pudding-like. Don't boil. Add butter and vanilla. Pour into a cooked pastry pie shell. Cool. Use egg whites to make meringue, or serve with whipped cream.

Recipe Note: Jill (McClelland) Russell is Program Manager for the Jackson Hole Historical Society & Museum. She was raised in Ohio. She got this recipe from her grandmother, Fannie McClelland. "This is an awesome dessert, rich and pudding-like," Jill says. "It's an old favorite from the Amish country of Ohio."

MOCK MINCE PIE

Happy Chambers Weston
Jackson Hole resident since she was 5 years old

2 eggs
2 crackers
½ c. vinegar
1 tsp. all kinds of spice
1 c. sugar

1 c. molasses
1 c. hot water
currants
raisins

Mix together and pour into uncooked pie shell. Bake until done.

9-Inch Pastry Crust

⅓ c. shortening
1 c. flour
½ tsp. salt

1 tsp. sugar
water

Cut shortening into flour, salt, and sugar mixture. Add water 1 teaspoon at a time until dough barely sticks together. Form into a ball, and roll out into shape needed. A tender, flaky crust depends on keeping dough chilled, using as little water as possible, and handling as little as possible

Recipe Note: This recipe was originally from a hand-written book dated 1886. Pioneer mince pie was a handy way to use scraps of meats and even vegetables. Dried fruit and molasses were added for sweetness. Happy Weston got this recipe from a friend's old cookbook. Try this at your own risk!

SADIE'S CARAMEL PIE

Sara Gibbs "Sadie" Weston
Member of the Pure Food Club

1 c. brown sugar
1 T. (good) flour wet with 1 c. milk

touch of butter
pinch of salt
3 egg yolks

This recipe has no directions as written in Genevieve Van Vleck's recipe book. Try mixing it all together and cooking to thicken.

Recipe Note: Sadie was Genevieve Van Vleck's best friend. "After Mother got the dishes done and house picked up," Jean Stewart remembers, "she'd slip into a clean dress and go to Auntie Weston's for a cup of tea. She took a short cut through Ma Reed's yard to her house near the present Back Porch store."

Pastry

RHUBARB CRISP

Leora Robertson
Jackson Hole resident since 1932

2½ c. rhubarb, cut in small pieces
⅔ c. granulated sugar
⅓ c. flour
¼ tsp. salt
½ tsp. cinnamon

1 c. brown sugar
1 c. Quick oatmeal
½ tsp. salt
¾ c. flour
¾ c. margarine
3 T. water

Mix together, and place in a 9 x 13-inch buttered baking pan: rhubarb, granulated sugar, ⅓ cup flour, ¼ teaspoon salt, and cinnamon. In another bowl, mix well 1 cup brown sugar, oatmeal, ½ teaspoon salt, ¾ cup flour, and margarine. Spread over rhubarb mixture as a topping. Then sprinkle 3 Tablespoons water over the top. Bake uncovered at 350° for 40 minutes.

Recipe Note: Leora Robertson got this recipe from former Jackson Hole resident Gloria Klingler, who now lives in Victor, Idaho. It is a tasty, easy dessert. Leora and her late husband Dell have six children, several of whom still live in the valley.

38140-01

BASIL TOMATO TART

Steve Newman
Moose Head Ranch chef

pie shell
1½ c. Mozzarella cheese
4 tomatoes
1 c. loose packed fresh basil

4 cloves garlic
½ c. mayonnaise
¼ c. Parmesan cheese
⅛ tsp. white pepper

Pre-bake pie shell. Sprinkle with ½ cup Mozzarella cheese. Cut tomatoes into wedges and drain on paper towels. Arrange atop melted cheese. In food processor, chop basil and garlic. Sprinkle over tomatoes. Mix together 1 cup Mozzarella cheese, mayonnaise, Parmesan cheese, and white pepper. Smooth over top of basil and tomatoes. Bake at 350° for 25-30 minutes until golden.

Recipe Note: This recipe was contributed by Louise Davenport, current owner of the Moose Head Ranch. It is from the files of ranch chef, Steve Newman, and is served to ranch guests.

PECAN PIE BARS

Jean Van Vleck Stewart
Jackson Hole resident since 1920

2 c. all-purpose flour
½ c. confectioners' sugar
1 c. butter or margarine,
  softened
1 14-oz. can sweetened
  condensed milk

1 egg
1 tsp. vanilla extract
pinch salt
1 6-oz. pkg. toffee-flavored
  chips
1 c. chopped pecans

In mixing bowl, combine flour and sugar. Cut in butter until mixture resembles coarse meal. Press firmly into a greased 9 x 13-inch pan at least 2 inches deep. Bake at 350° for 15 minutes. Meanwhile, in another bowl, beat milk, egg, vanilla, and salt. Stir in toffee chips and pecans. Spread evenly over baked crust. Bake for another 20-25 minutes or until lightly browned. Cool, then refrigerate. When thoroughly chilled, cut into bars. Store in refrigerator. Makes 4 dozen.

Recipe Note: Jean Stewart has wonderful memories of growing up in Jackson Hole. Her mother, Genevieve Van Vleck, was a member of the Pure Food Club, and Jean remembers her going to club meetings.

APPLE DANISH

Betty Benson
Jackson Hole resident since 1934

4 c. sifted flour
1 tsp. salt
1¾ c. butter-flavored Crisco
1 egg yolk, beaten
¾ c. milk
6 c. sliced apples

2 c. sugar
3 T. tapioca
½ cube butter
1 tsp. cinnamon
¼ tsp. salt
1 egg, slightly beaten

Cut together the flour, salt, and Crisco until finely textured. Mix beaten egg yolk and milk; add to flour mixture, and mix lightly. Roll out half in a jelly roll pan (with sides). Roll other half of dough for the top. For filling, mix apples, sugar, tapioca, butter, cinnamon, and salt. Spread over crust in pan. Top with rolled out dough. Close edges around jelly roll pan. Brush top with slightly beaten egg. Bake for 15 minutes at 425°. Reduce temperature to 375° and bake another 30 minutes. Glaze with a mixture of powdered sugar, salt, vanilla, and milk, while still hot.

Recipe Note: Betty Benson and husband Tommy have six grown children. She was Draft Board Clerk in the 1940s and secretary to County Attorney Wilford Neilson.

"The more you eat, the less flavor; the less you eat, the more flavor."
- Chinese Proverb

38140-01

Desserts

UPSIDE DOWN DATE PUDDING

Della Woodward
Moved to Jackson Hole in 1946

1½ c. pitted dates
3 c. light brown sugar
4½ T. butter
¾ c. granulated sugar
2 eggs

2¼ c. all-purpose flour
1½ tsp. baking soda
¾ tsp. baking powder
¾ tsp. salt
1½ c. chopped nuts

Combine dates and 1½ c. boiling water. Set aside and cool. In bowl, beat ¾ c. brown sugar, 3 tablespoons butter, 2 eggs, and ¾ c. granulated sugar. Add dates, flour, baking soda, baking powder, salt, and nuts. Mix well. Pour into a 9 x 12-inch greased pan. Mix remaining brown sugar, butter, and 2¾ c. boiling water, and pour over the batter. (That's right. It separates and looks odd, but do it anyway.) Bake uncovered at 375° for 40 minutes. When cooked the pudding/cake is on top with the dates, and the frosting is on the bottom. Spoon it out and serve warm, or cool. Top with whipped cream.

Recipe Note: Della moved to Jackson when she married Chet Woodward, a Jackson Hole native. Della retired from the County Clerk's office in 1991 after 15 years there. People often ask her to bring this delicious pudding/cake to potluck dinners. The Woodwards moved to Utah a few years ago.

STRAWBERRY RHUBARB CRUMBLE

Leesa Wilde
Jackson Hole resident since 1980

6 c. rhubarb, washed and cut
  into ¾-inch pieces
1 c. sugar
1 c. water

1 cube butter or margarine
1 lg. pkg. strawberry Jello
1 white or yellow cake mix

Lay rhubarb in bottom of ungreased 9 x 11-inch cake pan. Sprinkle sugar over rhubarb. Then sprinkle Jello over that. Pour water over rhubarb, sugar, and Jello layers. Sprinkle cake mix powder (unmixed) over top. Melt butter and drizzle over cake mix. Bake 50 minutes at 350°. Serve either hot or cooled with ice cream, whip cream, or other favorite topping.

Recipe Note: Leesa and husband Larry Wilde own and operate Creekside Meats, Market & Deli. Leesa got this recipe from her sister. It's a simple, delicious dessert. Rhubarb, one of the few plants that seems to thrive in Jackson Hole's often hostile climate, was a mainstay for early settlers.

PUMPKIN ROLL-UP

Karen Merrell
Jackson Hole resident since 1976

Roll:

4 eggs, beaten 5 minutes	2 tsp. cinnamon
1 c. pumpkin	$\frac{1}{2}$ tsp. salt
1$\frac{1}{3}$ c. sugar	1 tsp. baking powder
1 tsp. lemon juice	$\frac{1}{2}$ tsp. nutmeg
1 c. flour	chopped nuts

Cream Cheese Frosting:

1 c. powdered sugar	4 T. butter or hard margarine,
6 oz. cream cheese, softened	softened

Blend well and set aside: beaten eggs, pumpkin, sugar, and lemon juice. In another bowl, mix flour, cinnamon, salt, baking powder, and nutmeg. Add to egg mixture and blend well. Pour into greased jelly roll pan. Sprinkle with chopped nuts. Bake 15 minutes at 375°. Remove from oven and cool 2-3 minutes. Turn out onto tea towel dusted with powdered sugar (do not use paper towel, must be a cloth towel). While pumpkin roll is still warm, roll it up together with tea towel. Let cool. When cool, unroll gently. Remove towel. Make cream cheese frosting by mixing together powdered sugar, cream cheese, and butter. Spread over open pumpkin roll. Re-roll. Either frost or dust top with powdered sugar. Slice and serve.

Recipe Note: Karen got this recipe from a former Jackson Hole resident, Sylvia Harber. It has become a family favorite for Thanksgiving and Christmas desserts. Karen works for Teton County Schools. Her husband Gaylen works for the Sheriff's Department.

"Whatever will satisfy hunger is good food."

- Chinese Proverb

38140-01

RASPBERRY DELIGHT

Claudia Roylance
Moved to Jackson Hole in 1974

2 10-oz. pkgs. marshmallows
1 pt. whipping cream, whipped
2 pkgs. frozen raspberries

1 c. raspberry juice
1 pkg. vanilla wafers
1+ cube butter

Crush vanilla wafers. Mix with at least 1 cube butter. Make a layer of crumbs in bottom of baking pan. Reserve enough crumbs to sprinkle on top of mixture later. Melt marshmallows in large pan with raspberry juice. Add berries. Let cool. Fold in whipped cream. Pour over crumbs in pan, and sprinkle remaining vanilla wafer crumbs on top. Chill at least 12 hours.

Recipe Note: This recipe is from the collection of Claudia Roylance who passed away in 1997. She and husband Dick lived here during their retirement years. Claudia was a superb cook whose desserts were legendary. This makes a tart and tasty finale to any meal, summer or winter.

MRS. RAGGS' DATE PUDDING

Daisy Tucker
Jackson Hole native

1 c. chopped dates (22 dates)
1 tsp. soda
1 c. boiling water
1 well-beaten egg
1/4 c. coarsely chopped walnuts

1 1/2 c. cake flour
1 c. sugar
pinch of salt
3 T. softened shortening
1 tsp. vanilla

Dissolve soda in boiling water. Pour boiling water over dates and set aside to cool. In mixing bowl, cream together cake flour, salt, sugar, and shortening. To creamed mixture, add beaten egg, nuts, and vanilla. Stir together. Then add date mixture. Dough will be light in texture. Bake in a greased and lightly floured 9 x 13-inch cake pan at 375° for 25 minutes or until tests done. Serve warm with whipped cream.

Recipe Note: Daisy Tucker was born in Jackson Hole in 1910. She got this recipe from the cook in her college dormitory more than 70 years ago. Date Pudding was served every Sunday morning, after the girls in the dorm chopped dates. It took five pans of pudding to serve all the girls.

CARAMEL PUDDING

Genevieve Van Vleck
Member of the Pure Food Club

1 c. brown sugar
1 good (heaping) T. flour
1 c. milk

touch of butter
pinch of salt
3 egg yolks

Wet brown sugar and flour with milk. Add salt and egg yolks. Cook in double boiler, stirring frequently until thick. Add butter at the last.

Recipe Note: Genevieve Van Vleck was a member of the Town Council during Jackson's all-woman government. She loved to cook. Although Genevieve passed away many years ago, this recipe has become a family favorite. It is shared by her daughter Jean Stewart.

CHOCOLATE CRUNCH BROWNIES

Lois Jurich
Jackson Hole resident since 1957

1 c. margarine
2 c. sugar
2 tsp. vanilla
4 eggs
6 T. cocoa
1 c. flour

½ tsp. salt
1 7-oz. jar marshmallow creme
1 c. creamy peanut butter
2 c. milk chocolate chips
3-4 c. Rice Krispies

Cream margarine and sugar. Add eggs and vanilla. Stir in cocoa, flour, and salt. Spread in ungreased 9 x 13-inch pan. Bake at 350° for 30-35 minutes or until set. Cool. Drop spoonfuls of marshmallow cream over brownies and spread to edges of pan. Melt peanut butter and chocolate chips together. Stir in Rice Krispies, and spread over marshmallow layer. Store in refrigerator. Enjoy lots of calories!

Recipe Note: Lois and husband Arch Jurich retired from working in the Teton County School system in 1982. They spend their winters in Arizona. This recipe is rich and gooey, a delicious treat.

"I'm not crazy...I've just been in a bad mood for 40 years."
- Shirley MacLaine in Steel Magnolias

38140-01

CHOCOLATE PUDDING

Genevieve Van Vleck
Member of the Pure Food Club

1 oz. unsweetened chocolate
½ c. sugar
1 heaping T. cornstarch mixed
  with a little milk

1 beaten egg
2 c. milk
1 tsp. vanilla
1 T. butter or margarine

Melt chocolate; then stir in sugar in double boiler. Add cornstarch, egg, and milk. Mix well, and cook in double boiler until thickened. Add vanilla and butter when pudding thickens. Serve warm or cooled. Can be poured into a cooked pie shell.

Recipe Note: Genevieve Van Vleck was born in Lawton, Michigan, but moved to Jackson Hole in 1911 when she married her childhood sweetheart, Roy Van Vleck. Although Genevieve passed away many years ago, this recipe is still a family favorite. It was shared by her daughter, Jean Stewart.

SUET PUDDING

Genevieve Van Vleck
Member of the Pure Food Club

1 c. suet
1 c. seeded raisins
1 c. sour milk
1 tsp. cloves
1 c. sorghum molasses
1 c. flour

½ c. currants
1 tsp. cinnamon
1 egg
1 tsp. soda
½ tsp. salt

Mix together, pour into baking powder cans (about the size of large tomato juice cans) and steam in a steamer 2 hours.

Sauce:

1 c. maple syrup
1 c. sugar
1-3 c. butter
vanilla & nutmeg to taste if
  desired

3 T. flour
1 tsp. salt
1 qt. boiling water
2 T. wine or brandy

Boil 5 or 10 minutes

Recipe Note: This recipe was recorded on a slip of paper found in Genevieve's cookbook. She loved desserts. Genevieve was on Jackson's all-woman town council from 1920-1923. She was married to Roy Van Vleck who owned the Jackson Mercantile, an early Jackson general store.

MAPLE MOUSSE

Genevieve Van Vleck
Member of the Pure Food Club

1 c. bottled milk or ½ c. evaporated milk and ½ c. water

¾ c. maple OR cane and maple syrup

¼ c. granulated sugar

2 T. cornstarch

3 egg yolks

2 c. heavy cream

Heat milk in the top of a double boiler. Add the syrup to the sugar and cornstarch, which have been mixed together. Slowly add to the hot milk, stirring constantly. Cook over low heat for 15 minutes, stirring frequently. Add the beaten egg yolks and cook until smooth and thickened. Cool. Fold in the cream, which has been whipped stiff. Pour into a tray of an automatic refrigerator, turn control to coldest setting and freeze about 3 hrs. or until stiff, stirring once. Serves 8. To serve 3 or 4, may halve this recipe.

Recipe Note: This recipe, clipped from a magazine and stuffed into Genevieve's cookbook, says it was "tested by Good Housekeeping Institute." Genevieve loved to cook and enjoyed good food. As a town councilwoman, one of her priorities was to get a decent road up to the cemetery on Snow King.

Recipe Favorites

38140-01

Cakes, Cookies & Candies

Teton Lodge kitchen

Collection of the Jackson Hole Historical Society & Museum

Joe Ruby's Cafe in the new part of the Cowboy Bar
Charlotte Robertson and Heavy Dillion

Collection of the Jackson Hole Historical Society & Museum

38140-ca-7b

Cakes, Cookies & Candies

Cakes

ONE EGG CAKE

Maggie McBride
Member of the Pure Food Club

1 egg	2/3 c. sweet milk
1 T. butter	1 2/3 c. flour
1 c. sugar	2 tsp. baking powder

Sift flour and baking powder together. Cream egg, butter, and sugar. Add milk. Stir in dry ingredients. Bake in moderate oven (350°) until tests done. Instead of a whole egg, 2 yolks can be used in the cake, and the 2 egg whites can be used in the frosting.

Recipe Note: Maggie and her husband Jim McBride came to Jackson Hole by covered wagon in 1896. Maggie wrote that she adds a "trifle more flour" if she includes nuts. This cake may have been created when eggs and other commodities were rationed during World War I. The hand-written notes it was taken from were somewhat incomplete. Try this one at your own risk!

"There is nothing new except what is forgotten."

- Mlle. Bertin

FILLED FUDGE CAKE

Susie Nethercott
Jackson Hole native

2 c. sugar
2 eggs
1 c. buttermilk
¾ c. unsweetened cocoa
2 tsp. baking powder
1 c. hot water

1 c. canola oil
3 c. flour
1 tsp. vanilla
2 tsp. soda
1½ tsp. salt
1 c. chopped nuts (opt.)

Cream sugar, oil, and salt. Add eggs and vanilla. Mix together flour, baking powder, soda, and cocoa. Add to creamed mixture alternately with buttermilk and hot water. Mix well. Add nuts if desired. Grease well a large bundt or angel food cake pan. Pour ½ of batter into pan.

Filling:

¼ c. sugar
1 tsp. vanilla
8-oz. pkg. softened cream
  cheese

1 c. semi-sweet chocolate chips
½ c. coconut (opt.)

Mix all filling ingredients together well, and drop by spoonfuls on top of first layer of cake batter. Then cover with remaining batter. Bake at 350° for 1 hour. Do not turn out of pan until completely cool (3-4 hours). Turn out onto plate. Ice with thin chocolate glaze if desired.

Recipe Note: Susie Nethercott and husband Phill are both Jackson Hole natives. They own and operate Jackson Hole Air Freight. This cake is a favorite of their five children and extended family. It's plenty rich even without the chocolate glaze. If you like chocolate, you'll love this cake.

"When you teach your son, you teach your son's son."

- The Talmud

GEORGE WASHINGTON CAKE

Susie Nethercott
Jackson Hole native

1½ c. sugar
2⅔ c. cake flour, sifted
1 tsp. baking powder
1 tsp. vanilla
4 egg whites, beaten stiff

¾ c. Crisco
¼ tsp. salt
½ tsp. soda
1 c. buttermilk

Cream sugar and shortening until creamy and fluffy. Add vanilla. Sift dry ingredients together and add alternately with buttermilk, mixing after each addition. Beat egg whites until stiff, and fold into batter. Pour into greased 9 x 13-inch pan or two 9-inch round pans. Bake at 350° for 20 minutes or until tests done. Ice with fluffy white or cream cheese frosting.

Recipe Note: Susie got this recipe from her mother, Elaine Feuz, who taught many of the children of Jackson Hole music lessons years ago. This cake has become a family tradition for birthdays and holidays.

APRICOT BLOSSOM CAKE

Carol McCain
Jackson Hole resident since 1976

1 17-oz. can apricot halves
2+ c. flour
2 T. sugar
½ tsp. salt

1 pkg. dry yeast
⅓ c. milk
¼ c. margarine
1 egg

Drain apricot halves, reserving syrup. In a separate bowl, mix together: ½ cup flour, sugar, salt, and yeast. Combine milk, ⅓ cup apricot syrup, and margarine. Heat over low heat until liquids are very warm (120-130°F.) Add to dry ingredients, and beat 2 minutes at medium speed. Add ¼ cup flour and egg. Beat with mixer at high speed for 2 minutes. Add enough flour to make a stiff batter (about 1¼ cup). Cover. Refrigerate 2 hours to 2 days. Turn onto floured board. Roll into rectangle 10 inches x 18 inches. With doughnut cutter, cut 12 doughnuts. Arrange holes on greased baking sheet to form blossom center. Elongate the rings; arrange to form petals around center. Top petals and center with apricot halves. Cover. Let rise until double, about 1 hour. Bake at 375° about 20 minutes or until done. Cool. Drizzle with lemon confectioners' sugar icing.

Recipe Note: Carol McCain has been a 4-H leader for many years. She got this recipe from Kay Ellis, another 4-H leader. Kay lived in Jackson many years before moving to Victor, Idaho. This cake makes an elegant dessert for social functions. The McCain family has operated the Jenny Lake Boat dock in Grant Teton National Park for many years.

OVERNIGHT COFFEE CAKE

Lois Jurich
Jackson Hole resident since 1957

⅔ c. margarine
½ c. brown sugar
1 c. sugar
2 eggs
1 c. buttermilk
2 c. flour
1 tsp. baking powder
1 tsp. soda

½ tsp. salt
2 T. powdered milk
1 tsp. cinnamon
½ c. powdered sugar
½ tsp. cinnamon
½ c. nuts
¼ tsp. nutmeg

Cream margarine, brown sugar, and sugar. Beat eggs and add to creamed mixture. Then add buttermilk, flour, baking powder, soda, powdered milk, and 1 teaspoon cinnamon. Stir well. Pour mixture into 9 x 13-inch pan. Then mix the following together, and sprinkle over top of cake: powdered sugar, ½ teaspoon cinnamon, nuts, and nutmeg. Cover tightly and put in refrigerator overnight. Bake at 350° for 30 minutes or until done.

Recipe Note: Lois and her husband Arch retired from the Teton County School system in 1982. Arch, a Wyoming native, arrived in Jackson in 1947. They spend their winters in Arizona. This is a great make-ahead dessert or breakfast dish.

"Truth is shorter than fiction."

- Irving Cohen

38140-01

RHUBARB CAKE

Lily Linn
Jackson Hole resident for many years

2 c. flour
1 tsp. soda
1 tsp. cinnamon
¼ tsp. cloves
2 eggs
1½ c. sugar or ¾ c. honey

1 tsp. salt
¼ tsp. nutmeg
½ c. shortening
½ c. milk
2 c. rhubarb

Beat flour, soda, cinnamon, cloves, eggs, sugar or honey, salt, nutmeg, shortening, and milk two minutes with beaters in mixing bowl. Fold in 2 c. rhubarb, cut into ½-inch pieces. Pour batter into 9 x 13-inch greased and floured baking pan.

Topping:

¼ c. flour
⅓ c. brown sugar
¼ c. chopped nuts

3 T. butter
½ tsp. cinnamon

Mix all ingredients together and pour over batter in baking pan. Bake in 350° pre-heated oven 45 minutes to 1 hour, until rhubarb is cooked.

Recipe Note: Lily Linn married Jackson Hole native Gene Linn. They lived on the Lower Linn Ranch for many years on the west side of the valley before moving to Victor, Idaho. This recipe makes a quick birthday cake. It can be served hot or cold.

"Some people, no matter how old they get, never lose their beauty - they merely move it from their faces into their hearts."

- Martin Buxbaum

ORANGE SLICE CAKE

Mary May Linnell
Born on Mormon Row, now lives in Utah

Cake:

1 c. butter or margarine	3½ c. flour
2 c. sugar	½ lb. chopped dates
4 eggs	1 lb. orange slice candy (be
½ c. buttermilk	generous)
1 tsp. soda (dissolved in	1 c. coconut
buttermilk)	2 c. chopped nuts (walnuts or
½ tsp. salt	pecans)

Glaze:

½ c. orange juice	½ c. powdered sugar

Grease and flour bundt pan. Preheat oven to 275°. Chop dates, candy, and nuts. Mix with coconut and dredge in ½ cup of the flour. Cream butter, sugar, and eggs. Mix in 3 cups flour alternately with buttermilk (add lemon juice to milk to sour it if buttermilk isn't available). Add candy/nut mixture. Pour into bundt pan. Bake for 2 hours or until cake tests done. Mix orange juice and powdered sugar together to make glaze. While cake is still in pan, pour glaze over cake. Leave in pan until completely cool. Invert on plate until it falls out. If cake sticks in pan, put in 350° oven for 3 minutes.

Recipe Note: Mary May Linnell is the daughter of Lester I. and Melba Moulton May. Mary spent part of her youth living on Mormon Row. She was seriously burned in a school bus/sleigh accident one winter there. This cake is a family favorite. The recipe was contributed by Anna Bush and Clara May Bush, Mary's sister.

"Anything will give up its secrets if you love it enough."
- George Washington Carver

38140-01

POLKA DOT CAKE

Carolyn Mellor
Jackson Hole native

1¼ c. chopped dates
1 c. hot water
¾ c. butter or margarine
1 c. sugar
2 eggs
2 c. sifted flour

1 tsp. baking soda
½ tsp. salt
1 tsp. vanilla
1 6-oz. pkg. chocolate chips
½ c. chopped nuts

Mix dates and hot water; set aside to cool. Cream together butter and sugar; add eggs; beat until fluffy. Sift together flour, soda, and salt. Add to creamed mixture alternately with date mixture. Mix well after each addition. Stir in vanilla and ½ c. chocolate chips. Spread batter in a greased and floured 9 x 13-inch cake pan. Top with remainder of chocolate chips and nuts. Bake at 350° for 35 minutes. This cake does not need frosting.

Recipe Note: Carolyn and Norman Mellor III have three children. At one time, Norman's father was part-owner of the White Grass Ranch, now in Grand Teton National Park. Carolyn got this recipe from her mother, Lillian Robertson, who found it in an old farm magazine. It's been in the family for 30 years.

NEVER FAIL DRIPPER CAKE

Joyce Rudd
Jackson Hole resident since 1968

3 c. flour
2 c. sugar
1 c. oil
2 tsp. soda
1 c. buttermilk

1 tsp. vanilla
½ c. cocoa
1 tsp. salt
2 eggs
1 c. boiling water

Mix flour, sugar, soda, salt, eggs, oil, buttermilk, vanilla and cocoa all together. Add boiling water after mixing other ingredients well. Batter will be thin. Pour into a greased 9 x 13-inch cake pan. Bake at 350° for 35-40 minutes.

Recipe Note: Joyce baked this cake often for the crew and wranglers when the Rudd family operated Teton Trail Rides in Grand Teton National Park. It was one of their favorites, rich and moist.

DUTCH APPLE CAKE

Anna Rice Sanford
Mother of Eva Topping

1 c. flour
1/4 c. shortening
1 1/2 tsp. baking powder
4 T. sugar
1/2 tsp. nutmeg
1/2 tsp. salt

1/4 c. milk
1 egg
1/2 tsp. cinnamon
3 tart apples, peeled, cored, and
   sliced
melted butter

Mix together flour, shortening, baking powder, 1 Tablespoon sugar, nutmeg, salt, milk, egg, cinnamon, and apples. Pour into baking pan. Then add 3 Tablespoons sugar to melted butter, and sprinkle over top before baking. Bake 25-30 minutes in a preheated wood cookstove oven (probably about 350°).

Recipe Note: Anna Rice Sanford was one of the first, if not the first, white baby born in Wyoming. This old pioneer recipe seems a little short on sweetener to us. But since early settlers were hardy folks, maybe the amount listed was adequate. And we don't know how much butter. Try this one at your own risk!

WHITE CAKE

Sarah Gibbs "Sadie" Weston
Member of the Pure Food Club

scant 1 1/2 c. sugar
1/4 lb. butter (1/2 c.)
1 c. cold water

3 c. flour
3 tsp. baking powder
whites of 6 eggs

There were no written directions with this recipe. Take your best guess.

Recipe Note: Sadie Weston was Genevieve Van Vleck's best friend. Sadie had a beautiful head of curly hair. One side of it was gray; the other side was completely white. This recipe makes a delicious, light cake, according to Jean Van Vleck Stewart. Sadie's son Harry married Jean's sister Stella.

"If love is the answer, could you please rephrase the question?"
- Lily Tomlin

38140-01

BATTER CAKE

Genevieve Van Vleck
Member of the Pure Food Club

½ c. sugar
½ c. butter
4 egg yolks
4 T. milk

1 c. plus 1 T. flour
1 tsp. baking powder
1 tsp. vanilla
pinch salt

No instructions were included with this hand-written recipe. Use a normal cake mixing method and bake at an average temperature until cake tests done.

Recipe Note: Genevieve loved desserts. "Mother loved anything with cream and butter in it," Jean Stewart says. "Then her gall bladder would flare up, and the doctor would tell her, 'You've got to stop this.' She'd be good for a day or two, and then go right back to eating all the desserts."

LAYER CAKE

Marta "Wingie" Winger
Member of the Pure Food Club

1 c. sugar
½ c. butter (scant)
2 c. flour

2 tsp. baking powder
1 c. milk
flavor

No instructions were listed with this recipe. Consider using your usual directions for a from-scratch cake and baking in a moderate oven, from 350° to 375°.

Filling:

beaten whites of 2 eggs
1 c. sugar

⅓ c. water
1 square of chocolate

This filling also had no directions. We'd guess you'd melt the chocolate, and cook in a double boiler until ready to frost and fill cake, but take your best guess.

Recipe Note: Wingie served as the town clerk, appointed by Mayor Grace Miller in the all-woman government in Jackson. She and husband Dick moved to the valley in 1913. They tried homesteading up Flat Creek, but had no farming experience. Dick later bought the Jackson's Hole Courier.

ANGEL FOOD CAKE

Georgia Ely
Member of the Pure Food Club

1 c. well sifted flour
1½ c. sugar
whites of 12 eggs

1 tsp. cream of tartar
flavoring (vanilla perhaps)
pinch of salt

Sift flour six times, then measure out 1 cup to use in recipe. Beat eggs about half stiff. Put in cream of tartar. Then beat stiff. Add salt and flavoring. Fold in sugar and flour last of all. Bake 45 minutes. No oven temperature was listed with this recipe. We're guessing 375°.

Recipe Note: Georgia Ely lived close to Genevieve Van Vleck and often sewed for her.

FUNERAL CAKE

Erma Nethercott
Jackson Hole native born and raised on the Elk Refuge

3 c. sugar
1½ c. butter
1½ c. milk
6 eggs (separated)
3 c. flour

3 squares melted baking
  chocolate
3 tsp. vanilla
1½ c. chopped walnuts

Cream butter, sugar, and egg yolks. Add melted chocolate and vanilla. Mix well. Add milk and then flour. Mix well. Stir in nuts. Beat egg whites to a stiff peak and fold into batter. Pour into a greased floured cake pan, and bake at 375° for 35-40 minutes. Cool and frost with your favorite chocolate frosting. Erma sometimes poured 2 cups of chocolate chips and 1½ cups of walnuts on top of the batter before baking. It comes out gooey and delicious. Bake in large cake pan or three rounds for a layer cake.

Recipe Note: Erma got this recipe from her husband Moy's sister, Ethel Wilson. Erma's kids all called it "Aunt Ethel Cake." Every time someone died, Erma took this cake to their home or to the funeral luncheon. Over the years, Erma took it to so many funerals that it eventually became "Erma's Funeral Cake."

38140-01

QUICK DEVIL'S FOOD CAKE

Rena Petersen
Member of the Pure Food Club

1 c. sugar
1 c. sour milk
1⅓ c. flour
4 T. cocoa, level
5 T. melted shortening

1 tsp. soda
½ tsp. baking powder
little salt
1 egg

Bake 20-30 minutes. No oven temperature was given for this recipe. Consult a modern cookbook.

Frosting

3 T. cocoa
3 T. melted butter

3 T. hot coffee
powdered sugar

Mix together cocoa, butter, and coffee. Add enough powdered sugar to thicken. Spread over cooled cake.

Recipe Note: Rena Petersen was married to local outfitter, Frank Petersen. They lived across the street from Genevieve Van Vleck in the same house the Wingers had lived in. Rena took in girls who were nearing the end of their pregnancies and took care of them until they were ready to deliver.

"The best and most beautiful things in the world cannot be seen or even touched. They must be felt with the heart."

- Helen Keller

Cookies

BUTTERSCOTCH ICE BOX COOKIES

Alice Giles
Member of the Pure Food Club

2 c. brown sugar (or 1 c.
  white & 1 c. brown)
1 c. butter (not margarine)
1 scant tsp. soda
4 c. flour

1 tsp. vanilla
2 eggs
1 tsp. cream of tartar
1 c. chopped nuts

Cream sugars and butter. Add eggs, well beaten. Sift soda and cream of tartar with 1 cup flour. Add to creamed mixture. Then add nuts and vanilla. Add the rest of the flour, kneading the last of the flour into the mixture. Be sure to use all flour called for. Shape in rolls, and set in a cool place until morning. Slice and bake in a moderate oven (350°). Check cookies for doneness between 8 and 12 minutes. Unbaked cookie dough can be stored in refrigerator up to two weeks.

Recipe Note: Alice Giles had a shop on the south side of the Town Square, where she sold linens in the 1920s. Jean Stewart remembers her as a tiny woman. "Everybody loved her," Jean says. "Her husband gambled and gambled, and she worked and worked." These delectable butterscotch cookies were no doubt served at meetings of the Pure Food Club.

ICE BOX COOKIES

Joyce Rudd
Jackson Hole resident since 1968

1 lb. butter or margarine
1½ c. brown sugar
1½ c. white sugar
3 eggs
6 c. flour

1 tsp. soda
1 tsp. salt
1 T. vanilla
1 c. chopped nuts

Cream butter. Add sugar, eggs, and other ingredients. Mix well. Add any of the following singly or in combination: chocolate chips, raisins, dates, candied fruit, coconut, etc. and mix well. Roll dough into rolls in wax paper. Chill. Can be frozen. Slice and bake on an ungreased cookie sheet at 350° for 10 to 12 minutes or until lightly browned.

Recipe Note: The Rudd family operated Teton Trail Rides in Grand Teton National Park from 1950 to 1993. This recipe is popular with the Rudds' children and grandchildren.

38140-01

SOFT SUGAR COOKIES

Marge Ryan
Jackson Hole native born on Mormon Row

3½ c. flour
½ tsp. salt
½ c. shortening (Marge uses
  Crisco)
1 egg

1 c. sour milk (can add 1 T.
  vinegar to sweet milk)
1 tsp. soda
1 c. sugar
1 tsp. vanilla

Sift dry ingredients. Cream sugar, shortening, and egg. Add vanilla. Add dry ingredients. Mix well. Chill for about an hour. Then roll out to about ¼-inch thick, and cut with cookie cutter. Bake at 400° about 10-12 minutes. Do not overcook.

Recipe Note: This is one of Marge's grandchildren's favorite recipes. It's a great cookie to decorate for holidays. Marge worked at the local telephone company and at Jackson Drug for many years. She recently retired from her position as Teton County Elections Clerk.

HARVEST BARS

Shirlene Edwards Case
Jackson Hole resident for many years

½ c. raisins
2 T. flour
1 c. brown sugar
½ c. chopped nuts
½ c. melted margarine
⅔ c. pumpkin
2 eggs

½ tsp. baking powder
½ tsp. ginger
½ tsp. cinnamon
½ tsp. vanilla
½ c. flour
½ tsp. soda
½ tsp. nutmeg

Mix together and set aside raisins, 2 Tablespoons flour, brown sugar, chopped nuts, and margarine. In another bowl, stir together pumpkin, eggs, baking powder, ginger, cinnamon, vanilla, flour, soda, and nutmeg. Add this mixture to first ingredients and stir. Pour into greased baking pan. Bake at 325° for 20-25 minutes. Ice if desired.

Recipe Note: Shirlene moved to Jackson Hole in the early 1970s. She moved to Utah in the mid-1980s. This recipe was a family favorite when her three children were growing up in Jackson Hole.

ANGEL COOKIES

Myrtle Ward
Has lived in Jackson more than 20 years

3 eggs
¾ c. sugar
¾ tsp. vanilla

2 tsp. baking powder
1½ c. flour

Beat eggs until frothy. Add sugar, beating well. Sift flour with baking powder. Add slowly to egg mixture. Stir in vanilla. Drop half-teaspoons of batter onto greased cookie sheet 3 inches apart. Bake 5 minutes at 400°. Yields about 5 dozen cookies.

Recipe Note: Myrtle got this recipe from Gene Ridenour, a chef who used to own the Open Range, a cafe once located where Legacy Gallery is now. Gene was educated in France and operated a cooking school in Jackson at one time. This is a simple, quick recipe. The cookies can be decorated if desired.

MR. STEINER'S OATMEAL COOKIES

Chris Miller
Jackson Hole native

1 c. shortening
1 c. granulated sugar
1 c. brown sugar
2 eggs
1 tsp. vanilla

1 tsp. baking soda dissolved in
 1 T. water
2 c. flour
2 c. oatmeal, not Quick
½ tsp. cinnamon

Mix together shortening, sugars, eggs, and vanilla. Add baking soda and water. In another bowl, mix together flour, cinnamon and oatmeal. Stir dry ingredients into shortening mixture. Add raisins or chocolate chips if desired. Roll into balls, dip in sugar if desired, and flatten onto a greased cookie sheet. Bake at 350° for 10 minutes.

Recipe Note: Chris Miller, daughter of Man and Vi McCain and grand-daughter of A.C. "Mac" and Lily McCain, has been heavily involved in the family operation of Teton Boating in Grand Teton National Park for many years. Chris' daughter Carma got this recipe from her 2nd grade teacher, Mr. Steiner.

38140-01

CHOCOLATE DROP COOKIES

Vi McCain
Jackson Hole resident for more than 70 years

½ c. shortening
2 c. brown sugar
2 eggs
1½ c. buttermilk
4 c. flour

1 tsp. soda
4 squares of baking chocolate
  (melted)
2 tsp. vanilla

Cream together shortening and brown sugar. Mix in eggs, buttermilk, chocolate, vanilla, flour and soda. Drop by teaspoons onto a greased baking sheet. Bake at 350° for up to 10 minutes. Frost with your favorite quick fudge frosting while cookies are still hot.

Recipe Note: Vi McCain, who married Jackson Hole native Man McCain, got this recipe from her sister, Lucile Rock. This simple delicious cookie recipe was one of Vi's favorites. Vi and Lucile are granddaughters of Pap Deloney, who operated the first general store in Jackson Hole. Vi passed away in 2000.

RAISIN FILLED COOKIES

Melba Lucile Moulton May
Jackson Hole native grew up on Mormon Row

Filling:

1¼ c. ground raisins
¾ c. sugar
1 c. chopped nuts

1½ c. water
2 T. flour

Cookies:

1½ c. margarine
¾ c. brown sugar
¾ c. white sugar
3 eggs
3 T. cream or evaporated milk

1½ tsp. vanilla
1½ tsp. baking powder
1 tsp. baking soda
1 tsp. salt
4½ c. flour

For filling, bring raisins, water, sugar, and flour to a boil. Add nuts. Cool. For cookies, cream margarine and sugar. Blend in eggs, cream, and vanilla. Add dry ingredients, and mix well. Chill dough well, so a minimum of flour has to be used when rolling and cutting cookies. Cut dough into circles. Place a dollop of filling on half of circles, and cover with remaining dough circles. Pinch edges together. Bake at 350° for 10-12 minutes or until light brown.

Recipe Note: Melba May was married to former Jackson Mayor Lester I. May. She was the daughter of Mormon Row homesteaders T.A. and Lucile Blanchard Moulton. An excellent cook, Melba used to make these cookies for sledding parties and other special occasions. Contributed by daughter Clara May Bush.

PUMPKIN COOKIES

Stacey Smith
Jackson Hole resident since 1994

½ c. shortening
1½ c. sugar
1 egg
1 c. pumpkin
1½ c. flour
1 tsp. cinnamon

1 tsp. baking soda
1 tsp. baking powder
½ tsp. salt
1 tsp. vanilla
1 tsp. nutmeg
chocolate chips (opt.)

Stir shortening to soften; add sugar gradually. Cream together until light and fluffy. Add egg and mix well. Sift all dry ingredients, and add to creamed mixture, alternating with pumpkin. Beat well until smooth. Add vanilla and chocolate chips, if desired. Drop on greased cookie sheet. Bake at 375° for 10 minutes. Frost if desired.

Cream Cheese Frosting:

1 8-oz. pkg. cream cheese
2 tsp. vanilla

¼ c. butter
1 box powdered sugar

Mix cream cheese, vanilla, butter, and powdered sugar well, frost cookies, and enjoy.

Recipe Note: Stacey got this recipe from her mother. It's a delicious way to use leftover pumpkin from Halloween. Stacey moved to the valley from Afton, Wyoming and works at the Antler Motel.

"The trouble with America is that there are far to many wide-open spaces surrounded by teeth."

- Charles Luckman

GLAZED FRESH APPLE COOKIES

Chris Miller
Jackson Hole native

2 c. sifted flour	1 c. dark or light raisins
½ c. shortening	¼ c. apple juice or milk
1 tsp. salt	1 tsp. baking soda
1 tsp. cloves	1⅓ c. brown sugar
1 egg, unbeaten	1 tsp. cinnamon
1 c. finely chopped unpeeled apples	½ tsp. nutmeg
	1 c. nuts, chopped (opt.)

Combine flour and baking soda. Mix shortening, brown sugar, salt, cinnamon, cloves, nutmeg, and egg until well blended. Stir in half of flour mixture, then nuts, apples, and raisins. Blend in apple juice and remaining flour mixture. Drop rounded tablespoons of dough on greased cookie sheet. Bake 11 to 14 minutes at 350°.

Vanilla Glaze:

1½ c. powdered sugar	⅛ tsp. salt
1 T. soft butter or margarine	2½ T. canned milk or cream
¼ tsp. vanilla	

Mix together and spread over cookies while warm.

Recipe Note: This is a Deloney family recipe Chris got from her Aunt Clair Deloney Jay. Chris' mother, Vi Deloney McCain and Clair are both granddaughters of Charles "Pap" Deloney who owned Jackson Hole's first general store in the early 1900s.

OATMEAL COOKIES

Marge Ryan
Jackson Hole native born on Mormon Row

1 c. raisins	2 c. flour
1 c. water	¾ tsp. soda
1 c. Crisco	1 tsp. salt
1 c. sugar	1½ c. uncooked Quick oats
2 eggs	½ c. broken walnuts
1 tsp. vanilla	

Cook raisins and water together until raisins are soft, about 10 minutes. Drain juice off raisins and save for later. Let cool to room temperature. Meanwhile, cream together Crisco, sugar, and eggs. Stir in 5 Tablespoons of the raisin liquid and vanilla. Sift together and stir in: flour, soda, and salt. Add oats, cooked raisins, and nuts. Mix well, and drop onto greased cookie sheet. Bake at 400° for 12 minutes. If your family doesn't like raisins, substitute chocolate chips.

Recipe Note: Marge got this recipe from her mother-in-law, Lyle Crisp. It has been in the family for many years and is a favorite.

BEST SUGAR COOKIES

Marilyn Nelson
Jackson Hole Resident since 1968

1 c. butter (not margarine)
2 c. sugar
3 eggs
1 c. sour cream
1 tsp. vanilla

5 c. flour
4 tsp. baking powder
1 tsp. soda
½ tsp. salt

Cream butter and sugar. Add eggs, sour cream, and vanilla. Sift soda, flour, baking powder, and salt together, and add to creamed mixture. Refrigerate overnight. Roll out and cut into shapes. Bake at 350° for 8 minutes or until light brown. Cool and frost if desired.

Recipe Note: Marilyn Nelson, who works at Knobe's, uses this recipe to bribe family members as needed. Try them; they may work for you, too.

ALTA'S CHOCOLATE DROP COOKIES

Alta Webb
Jackson Hole resident for many years

¼ c. fat
1 c. brown sugar
1 egg, well beaten
½ c. milk
1½ c. flour

½ tsp. soda
2 squares melted chocolate
1 c. chopped nuts
1 tsp. vanilla

Cream sugar, fat, and egg. Add milk and melted chocolate. Sift flour and soda together, and add to creamed mixture. Add chopped nuts and vanilla. Mix well. Drop by spoonfuls onto a greased tin. Bake in a moderately hot oven.

Recipe Note: This handwritten recipe was found in an old family cookbook belonging to the late Alta Webb. Alta was a superb cook, and these cookies were one of her specialties.

"You know you're old when the candles cost more than the cake."
- Bob Hope

PEARL'S COOKIES

Pearl Van Vleck
If not a member, probably attended some meetings of of the Pure Food Club

1 c. sugar	little nutmeg
½ c. butter	1 tsp. soda
½ c. sour cream	flour
1 egg	

Roll well with flour. These are the only instructions given with this recipe. However, we assume you would cream butter and sugar. Add egg, nutmeg, and soda, and enough flour to form a fairly stiff dough. Roll well with flour. These sound like a refrigerator cookie that can be sliced off and baked. Try this one at your own risk!

Recipe Note: Pearl was married to Roy Van Vleck's brother Frank. They lived on a ranch at the mouth of the Hoback River.

Candies

CANDY

Fannie Bean
Member of the Pure Food Club

½ c. white Karo	1 tsp. vanilla
1 c. sugar	⅓ c. nuts
1½ c. cream	

Put sugar, Karo syrup, and ½ cup cream in sauce pan. Cook until it forms a soft ball in water. Add ½ cup cream, and cook until it again forms a soft ball. Then add final ½ cup of cream and cook until it forms a soft ball in water again. Add vanilla and nuts. Pour into buttered pans to harden.

Recipe Note: Fannie Bean lived across the street from what is now the Sweetwater Restaurant. Because they lived at the top of the slope, it was called Beans Hill. Fannie was famous for her candy. This recipe is delicious and rich.

HOLIDAY PEPPERMINT CANDIES

Laraine McCollum
Jackson Hole resident since 1965

4 oz. cream cheese, softened
1 T. margarine
1 T. light corn syrup
¼ tsp. peppermint extract

4 c. powdered sugar
red and green food coloring
powdered sugar

Beat cream cheese, margarine, corn syrup, and peppermint in a large mixing bowl at medium speed with electric mixer until well-blended. Gradually add 4 c. powdered sugar. Mix well. Divide mixture into thirds. Knead a few drops green food coloring into one and red into another. Leave one uncolored. Wrap each third in plastic wrap. Working with one color at a time, shape into ¾-inch balls. Place on wax-paper-lined cookie sheet. Flatten each with the bottom of a glass dunked in powdered sugar. Repeat with each color mixture. You can also press mixture into small holiday molds if desired. Be sure to dust powdered sugar into molds before filling. Refrigerate. Makes 5 dozen.

Recipe Note: Laraine printed this recipe in one of her published cookbooks. Because it is so easy, it's a great way to let children help with making holiday treats. Other flavors, such as orange, with appropriate food colors, can be used for variety. Store each flavor separately.

HOLIDAY TAFFY

Susie Nethercott
Jackson Hole native

2 c. sugar
½ c. vinegar

⅓ c. light corn syrup
3 T. butter

Mix all ingredients together in heavy pan and bring to a boil. Cook to 260° on candy thermometer. For variety, add food colorings and/or flavorings. Pour onto a buttered cookie sheet or marble board. Butter hands. Stretch and pull taffy as quickly as possible until it becomes hard enough to break. Wrap and share with loved ones at Christmas time.

Recipe Note: Susie used this taffy recipe often for parties when her children were growing up. It's a great recipe for children to help create Christmas gifts from the kitchen.

38140-01

CHOCOLATE SPOONS

Junior Girl Scout Troop #264/Debby Hodges

1 bag chocolate chips
holiday or colored sprinkles
plastic spoons

plastic wrap
ribbons

Melt chocolate chips in double boiler or microwave. Dip plastic spoons in melted chocolate. Coat, front and back, partway up handle. Decorate with holiday or colored sprinkles. Let cool on wax paper, or set up in refrigerator or freezer. Wrap in plastic wrap and tie with a ribbon. Use spoons in hot chocolate to add extra flavor.

Recipe Note: This recipe is a great way for children to help make holiday gifts for teachers or friends.

HOLIDAY CARAMELS

Marge Ryan
Jackson Hole native born on Mormon Row

4 c. heavy whipping cream
4 c. sugar
3 c. white Karo syrup

4 cubes margarine
4 tsp. vanilla
3 c. chopped walnuts

Mix together in a heavy pan: 2 cups cream, sugar, Karo syrup, and margarine. Bring to a boil. Then add the other 2 cups cream. Cook over medium to low heat to firm ball stage. Remove from stove. Add vanilla and nuts. Pour into a shallow buttered pan and cool. Cut into squares.

Recipe Note: While this is a great holiday recipe, it's good any time of the year. "This recipe has been in my family as long as I can remember," Marge says. "We always had good thick cream on the ranch, but the heavy whipping cream you buy in the store works as well. This candy goes in a lot of my Christmas gifts."

"Age does not protect you from love. But love, to some extent, protects you from age."

- Jeanne Moreau

HOLIDAY ENGLISH CARAMELS

Sharon Nethercott
Jackson Hole native

1½ c. brown sugar, firmly
  packed
2 c. granulated sugar
2 c. dark Karo corn syrup

3 c. heavy whipping cream
2 c. walnuts, chopped
½ tsp. salt
3 T. butter

Mix all ingredients, except butter and nuts, in a large cooking pan. It boils up a lot, so allow plenty of room. Cook to firm ball stage or 245°F. It takes a while. Remove from heat, and add butter and nuts. Pour into buttered pan. Cool, cut into squares, and eat. If any are left, wrap for holiday gifts or freeze for later. To make popcorn balls or caramel corn with this recipe, just pour the cooked caramel mixture, including nuts, over about 2 gallons of popped corn. Form into balls or pull apart.

Recipe Note: Though Sharon was born in Jackson in the old St. John's Hospital between Glenwood and Cache, she was raised in Bondurant, Wyoming. She married Jackson Hole native Neal Nethercott. "These are the best caramels you will ever eat," Sharon says. "It's the first candy I learned to make on the ranch."

ALMOND JOYS

Donna Clark
Jackson Hole native

1 10-oz. bag sweetened coconut
1 can sweetened condensed
  milk

1 6-8-oz. bag unsalted almonds
2 c. chocolate chips
⅓ stick paraffin wax

Mix coconut and condensed milk well. Refrigerate until cold, at least 1 hour. Butter hands, and roll mixture into balls, with an almond in the middle of each. Freeze 1 to 2 hours. Meanwhile, melt chocolate and paraffin wax, stirring until smooth. Stick a toothpick into each ball, and dip into chocolate/wax mixture. Place on wax paper or in candy cups after dipping. Refrigerate to store, or use as gifts.

Recipe Note: Donna Clark has lived in the valley all her life. This recipe is her father, Don Clark's favorite Christmas candy. It's delicious and fairly simple. To make Mounds, just use semi-sweet chocolate chips and omit almonds. Donna works in the Teton County Clerk's Office.

PEANUT BRITTLE

Connie Hurley
Jackson Hole native

1 c. sugar
2 cubes Imperial Margarine (use Imperial only)

¼ c. water
1 c. dry roasted peanuts

Combine sugar, margarine, and water in a deep fry pan. Cook on medium high heat, stirring constantly with a wooden spoon. Boil and stir until mixture appears sudsy. Then cook about 5 more minutes until mixture starts to turn brown and caramelize. Add peanuts, or use any other kind of peanuts or other nuts you like. Cashews work well. Pour onto ungreased cookie sheet or marble slab. Let set up for 10-15 minutes until cooled. Break into chunks, and eat or share with friends.

Recipe Note: Connie Hurley's grandmother is Bea Ballew, and her great-grandfather was George Washington Kelly, for whom Kelly Street in Jackson was named. After he moved his family to town from the town of Kelly, he built a barn first, and his family lived there while he built them a house.

SPUDS CANDIES

Ann Bates
Jackson Hole resident for a number of years

2 cubes butter
2 c. powdered sugar
1 12-oz. pkg. milk chocolate chips

4 c. mini marshmallows
1 c. pecan pieces
coconut flakes

Melt butter and chocolate chips. Add powdered sugar and cream together. Pour mixture over marshmallows and nuts. Mix thoroughly. Put in refrigerator for 2 hours. Spoon out on waxed paper that is covered with coconut flakes. Form into balls. Let stand in refrigerator until well chilled.

Recipe Note: Ann Bates and husband Jan own and operate the Teton Steakhouse.

"Not a shred of evidence exists in favor of the idea that life is serious.
- Brendan Gil

MRS. DAVIS' PRALINES

Lokey Lytjen
Jackson Hole resident since 1993

3½ c. sugar   1 stick oleo
1 c. milk   3 c. pecans

In a small skillet or heavy saucepan, brown ½ cup sugar. In a large saucepan, mix milk and remaining sugar and heat to boiling. When this mixture begins to boil and the half-cup of sugar is brown and melted, remove from heat and combine in the large saucepan. While stirring, replace on stove burner. Begin timing when it begins to boil. Cook ten minutes over medium heat. Remove from heat, and add margarine. Let cook about five minutes, and then beat by hand until it begins to thicken (when spoon leaves a definite trail in the bottom of the pan). Add nuts and drop by spoonfuls onto foil, stirring from bottom of pan to keep the nuts distributed. When cool, the foil peels off easily. Cooking times may vary at higher altitudes.

Recipe Note: Lokey got this recipe from her best friend's mother when she was growing up in Savannah, Georgia. Mrs. Davis brought Lokey's family a plate stacked high with these pralines every Christmas afternoon. They looked forward to them every holiday. Mrs. Davis still brings the family this Christmas treat.

Recipe Favorites

38140-01

This
&
That

At the T. Lloyd hunting camp

Collection of the Jackson Hole Historical Society & Museum

38140-ca-8

Stephen N. Leek on Jackson Lake with Mackinaw

Collection of the Jackson Hole Historical Society & Museum

38140-ca-8b

This & That

CROCK POT APPLE BUTTER

Della Woodward
Jackson resident since 1946

6 c. apple pulp
3 c. sugar
2 tsp. cinnamon

1 tsp. ground cloves
¼ c. vinegar

Make apple pulp by cutting up apples, cooking them in water until tender, and running them through a sieve or colander. Mix pulp and all other ingredients in crock pot, and cook on high setting 4 hours. Remove lid, and cook 2 to 4 hours more, stirring occasionally. Put in sterilized jars and seal.

Recipe Note: Della grew up in Nebraska, but moved to Jackson Hole when she married Chet Woodward. Although this apple butter takes a long time to cook, it is delicious, requires little attention, and keeps the stove top clean. The Woodwards moved to Utah several years ago.

GRAVEYARD STEW

Clara May Bush
Jackson Hole native born on Mormon Row

1-2 o. milk per person
Butter, at least 1 pat per person
salt & pepper to taste

1-4 slices toasted bread per person

Heat milk on stove, almost to a scald. Add butter to taste, or allow each person to add their own. Pour hot milk into cereal bowls and serve with toast. Have each person salt and/or pepper their milk, tear toast into bite-size pieces, and drop it into their bowl. Let toast soak to desired sogginess, and eat with a spoon.

Recipe Note: Clara says her family had this stew, sometimes called Hot Milk Toast, several times a month when she was growing up on the May ranch. It was often served as a Sunday night supper or as a comfort food. Her grandfather, James Henrie May, an early home-steader, liked his made with cold milk.

"To eat is human; to digest, divine."

- Charles Townsend Copeland

PRIZE-WINNING CORNBREAD STUFFING

Carol Cavaner
Has lived in the valley in the 1990s

2 c. chopped, peeled, raw sweet
potatoes
1 c. chopped onion
1 c. sliced celery
1 T. snipped cilantro
1 tsp. ground ginger

5 c. coarsely crumbled
cornbread
¼ c. margarine or butter
2-4 T. chicken broth
¼ c. chopped walnuts

In a large skillet, cook sweet potatoes, onion, and celery in hot margarine or butter for 5-7 minutes or till just tender. Spoon mixture into a large mixing bowl. Stir in cilantro and ginger. Add cornbread and walnuts. Toss gently to coat. Add enough chicken broth to moisten. Use to stuff one 8-10 pound bird, or bake uncovered in a casserole dish at 375° about 45 minutes or till heated through. Makes about 6 cups stuffing (10 servings).

Recipe Note: Carol Cavaner moved to Jackson in 1997. Carol won a $100 prize for this recipe she created for a magazine contest in 1994. You can use leftover cornbread or bake a package of cornbread mix for this Southern-style stuffing.

ANOTHER GRAVEYARD STEW

Paula Leisinger
Jackson Hole resident since 1953

milk
eggs

toast
salt & pepper

Scald milk in a pan. Meanwhile, toast and butter bread, putting an extra pat of butter in the middle of the toast. Poach two eggs per person in milk. Place toast in a shallow bowl. Then spoon out the two poached eggs onto the toast. Pour hot milk over them. Season to taste with salt and pepper. Serve while warm.

Recipe Note: Paula worked as a nurse at St. John's Hospital when it was located between Glenwood and Cache streets. This dish was a favorite to make for breakfast or in the early hours of the morning when Paula and her friends had been out late caroling or on a hay ride. Paula's husband is Louis Leisinger.

HOMEMADE SOAP

Grace Miller
Member of the Pure Food Club

1 can of Red Seal Lye
4½ c. cold water
10 c. of grease

1 T. carbolic acid
1 tsp. sassafras
1 T. ammonia

Pour water on lye. Let it dissolve. When grease is luke warm, pour lye in slowly. Do not stir too long.

Recipe Note: This recipe was written in an old cookbook. Women of the day obviously knew more about the methods of soap making than we do today, as instructions are pretty vague. If you need more complete directions, check in with Roma Walker, who made soap for years.

ELEPHANT STEW

Susie Nethercott
Jackson Hole native

1 medium-sized elephant
2 rabbits (opt.)

salt and pepper

Cut elephant into small, bite-sized pieces. Add enough brown gravy to cover. Cook over kerosene fire about 4 weeks at 465°. This will serve 3,800 people. If more are expected, the two rabbits may be added. But do this only in an emergency. Most people do not like hare in their stew.

Recipe Note: Susie got this recipe from her sister Linda. It is originally from Tarzan and Jane.

CHILI SAUCE

Alta Webb
Jackson Hole resident for many years

a milk pan full of vine-ripened
  tomatoes
4 good-sized onions
1 tsp. ground cloves
1 tsp. all-spice

½ tsp. cinnamon
2 T. salt
6 T. sugar
1 pt. vinegar

Peel and cut up tomatoes and onions. Add cloves, all-spice, cinnamon, salt, sugar, and vinegar. Cook 1½ to 2 hours.

Recipe Note: This recipe was found in an old family cookbook belonging to the late Alta Webb. She and husband Clarence Webb are Clarene Law's parents. This chili sauce was a family favorite.

GRUEL

Happy Chambers Weston
Jackson Hole resident since she was 5 years old

1 pt. boiling water
3-4 lg. spoonfuls of nicely sifted
  oatmeal, rye, or Indian
  (cornmeal)
cold water

raisins
salt
white sugar
nutmeg

Boil pint of water in a large skillet. Stir up to 3 or 4 large spoonfuls of grain into cold water. (Recipe doesn't say how much. Just guess.) Pour cold water mixture into skillet while water is boiling. Let boil 8-10 minutes. Throw in a large handful of raisins to boil, if the patient is well enough to bear them. When put in a bowl, add a little salt, sugar, and nutmeg.

Recipe Note: You've probably always wanted a good gruel recipe to feed your sick loved ones. This one is from 1833, courtesy of Happy Weston's friend's old cookbook.

BREAD AND BUTTER PICKLES

Berla Stevens Chambers
Possible member of the Pure Food Club

14 medium cucumbers
2 onions
1 pt. vinegar
1 tsp. celery seed

1 tsp. white mustard seed
1 c. brown sugar
¼ tsp. turmeric powder
¼ c. salt

Boil vinegar, sugar, and spices together. Add other ingredients, and boil half an hour. Put in clean bottles, and seal.

Recipe Note: About 1912, Berla Stevens Chambers and husband Jim homesteaded on what is now the Elk Refuge. After selling their house on the Elk Refuge, they built a house which stood where the parking lot of the jail is now. He went to work for the government, putting up hay for elk on the Elk Ranch by hand.

"Dieting: A system of starving yourself to death so you can live a little longer."

- Jan Murray

38140-01

HOMEMADE NOODLES

Alta Webb
Jackson Hole resident for many years

2 eggs, well beaten
2 T. cream
1/2 T. baking powder

1/2 tsp. salt
flour

Blend cream, eggs, baking powder, and salt. Mix well, and add flour to make a stiff dough. Roll out on floured counter, and let dry. Cut into noodle-sized strips. Add to boiling broth or soup. Simmer until tender.

Recipe Note: Alta Webb, Clarene Law's mother, passed away several years ago. Alta was a wonderful cook. This recipe was handwritten in a small family cookbook.

HORSE RADISH SAUCE

Genevieve Van Vleck
Member of the Pure Food Club

1 sm. pkg. lemon Jello
1 c. boiling water
1/2 tsp. salt

2 T. vinegar or lemon juice
3/4 c. horse radish
1 c. cream, whipped

Dissolve Jello in boiling water. Add vinegar and salt. Chill. When slightly chilled, add horse radish, fold in whipped cream, and turn into a mold if desired. Chill until firm. Serve with baked ham, roast beef, turkey, or other meats.

Recipe Note: Genevieve got this recipe from her friend Emma Beam from Michigan. This sauce is part of a holiday tradition. While other family members claimed credit for originating this recipe, we have it on good authority that it came from Emma.

"Stomachs shouldn't be waist baskets."

- P.K. Thomajan

Recipe Favorites

38140-01

INDEX OF RECIPES

HUNGRY WRANGLERS'	
CASSEROLE	34
PORK CHOP CASSEROLE	34
STUFFED GREEN PEPPERS	35
STUFFED JUMBO SHELLS	36
TACO MEAT CASSEROLE	35
TATER TOT CASSEROLE	37
TURKEY BROCCOLI	
CASSEROLE	38
WESTERN HOSPITALITY	
CASSEROLE	37

Meat, Poultry, Fish & Wild Game

Meat

BARBECUED RIBS	40
BBQ BRISKET	39
PAN BROILED STEAK	39
VEGETABLE MEATBALLS	40

Poultry

CHICKEN LINDA	42
SMOKED HOLIDAY TURKEY	41
TETON CHICKEN	41

Fish

CRAB CAKES	43
CREAM OF CABBAGE SOUP	
WITH FISH	42
ETOUFEE (SHRIMP OR	
CRAYFISH)	44
ORANGE ROUGHY PARMESAN	44
SHRIMP PASTA SALAD	43
TUNA WALNUT FETTUCCINE	45

Wild Game

STROGANOFF	45
WILD GAME CASSEROLE	46

Pies, Pastry & Desserts

Pies

BEST COCONUT CREAM PIE	48
FROZEN PUMPKIN PIE	48
LEMON PIE FILLING	47
MOCK MINCE PIE	49
MY GRANDMA'S CHOCOLATE	
PIE	49
RHUBARB MERINGUE PIE	47

SADIE'S CARAMEL PIE	50

Pastry

APPLE DANISH	52
BASIL TOMATO TART	51
PECAN PIE BARS	51
RHUBARB CRISP	50

Desserts

CARAMEL PUDDING	56
CHOCOLATE CRUNCH	
BROWNIES	56
CHOCOLATE PUDDING	57
MAPLE MOUSSE	58
MRS. RAGGS' DATE PUDDING	55
PUMPKIN ROLL-UP	54
RASPBERRY DELIGHT	55
STRAWBERRY RHUBARB	
CRUMBLE	53
SUET PUDDING	57
UPSIDE DOWN DATE PUDDING	53

Cakes, Cookies & Candies

Cakes

ANGEL FOOD CAKE	68
APRICOT BLOSSOM CAKE	61
BATTER CAKE	67
DUTCH APPLE CAKE	66
FILLED FUDGE CAKE	60
FUNERAL CAKE	68
GEORGE WASHINGTON CAKE	61
LAYER CAKE	67
NEVER FAIL DRIPPER CAKE	65
ONE EGG CAKE	59
ORANGE SLICE CAKE	64
OVERNIGHT COFFEE CAKE	62
POLKA DOT CAKE	65
QUICK DEVIL'S FOOD CAKE	69
RHUBARB CAKE	63
WHITE CAKE	66

Cookies

ALTA'S CHOCOLATE DROP	
COOKIES	76
ANGEL COOKIES	72
BEST SUGAR COOKIES	76
BUTTERSCOTCH ICE BOX	
COOKIES	70
CHOCOLATE DROP COOKIES	73
GLAZED FRESH APPLE	
COOKIES	75
HARVEST BARS	71

Candies

This & That

How to Order

Get your additional copies of this cookbook by returning an order form and your check or money order to:

Teton Views Publishing
P.O. Box 832
Jackson Hole, WY 83001
(307) 733-7161
www.tetonviews.com

Please send me _____ copies of **Historical Recipes from the Pure Food Club of Jackson Hole & More** at **$12.95** per copy and **$2.50** for shipping and handling per book. Wyoming residents add 6% sales tax. Enclosed is my check or money order for $_____.

Mail Books To:

Name _____

Address _____

City _____ State _____ Zip _____

- -

Please send me _____ copies of **Historical Recipes from the Pure Food Club of Jackson Hole & More** at **$12.95** per copy and **$2.50** for shipping and handling per book. Wyoming residents add 6% sales tax. Enclosed is my check or money order for $_____.

Mail Books To:

Name _____

Address _____

City _____ State _____ Zip _____

38140-lb

Cooking Tips

1. After stewing a chicken, cool in broth before cutting into chunks; it will have twice the flavor.

2. To slice meat into thin strips, as for stir-fry dishes, partially freeze it so it will slice more easily.

3. A roast with the bone in will cook faster than a boneless roast. The bone carries the heat to the inside more quickly.

4. When making a roast, place dry onion soup mix in the bottom of your roaster pan. After removing the roast, add 1 can of mushroom soup and you will have a good brown gravy.

5. For a juicier hamburger, add cold water to the beef before grilling (½ cup to 1 pound of meat).

6. To freeze meatballs, place them on a cookie sheet until frozen. Place in plastic bags. They will stay separated so that you may remove as many as you want.

7. To keep cauliflower white while cooking, add a little milk to the water.

8. When boiling corn, add sugar to the water instead of salt. Salt will toughen the corn.

9. To ripen tomatoes, put them in a brown paper bag in a dark pantry, and they will ripen overnight.

10. To keep celery crisp, stand it upright in a pitcher of cold, salted water and refrigerate.

11. When cooking cabbage, place a small tin cup or can half full of vinegar on the stove near the cabbage. It will absorb the odor.

12. Potatoes soaked in salt water for 20 minutes before baking will bake more rapidly.

13. Let raw potatoes stand in cold water for at least a half-hour before frying in order to improve the crispness of French-fried potatoes. Dry potatoes thoroughly before adding to oil.

14. Use greased muffin tins as molds when baking stuffed green peppers.

15. A few drops of lemon juice in the water will whiten boiled potatoes.

16. Buy mushrooms before they "open." When stems and caps are attached firmly, mushrooms are truly fresh.

17. Do not use metal bowls when mixing salads. Use wood, glass or china.

18. Lettuce keeps better if you store it in the refrigerator without washing it. Keep the leaves dry. Wash lettuce the day you are going to use it.

19. Do not use soda to keep vegetables green. It destroys Vitamin C.

20. Do not despair if you oversalt gravy. Stir in some instant mashed potatoes to repair the damage. Just add a little more liquid in order to offset the thickening.

Copyright © 1999
Cookbooks by Morris Press

Herbs & Spices

Acquaint yourself with herbs and spices. Add in small amounts, ¼ teaspoon for every 4 servings. Crush dried herbs or snip fresh ones before using. Use 3 times more fresh herbs if substituting fresh for dried.

Basil
Sweet, warm flavor with an aromatic odor. Use whole or ground. Good with lamb, fish, roast, stews, ground beef, vegetables, dressing and omelets.

Bay Leaves
Pungent flavor. Use whole leaf but remove before serving. Good in vegetable dishes, seafood, stews and pickles.

Caraway
Spicy taste and aromatic smell. Use in cakes, breads, soups, cheese and sauerkraut.

Chives
Sweet, mild flavor like that of onion. Excellent in salads, fish, soups and potatoes.

Cilantro
Use fresh. Excellent in salads, fish, chicken, rice, beans and Mexican dishes.

Curry Powder
Spices are combined to proper proportions to give a distinct flavor to meat, poultry, fish and vegetables.

Dill
Both seeds and leaves are flavorful. Leaves may be used as a garnish or cooked with fish, soup, dressings, potatoes and beans. Leaves or the whole plant may be used to flavor pickles.

Fennel
Sweet, hot flavor. Both seeds and leaves are used. Use in small quantities in pies and baked goods. Leaves can be boiled with fish.

Ginger
A pungent root, this aromatic spice is sold fresh, dried or ground. Use in pickles, preserves, cakes, cookies, soups and meat dishes.

Herbs & Spices

Marjoram   May be used both dried or green. Use to flavor fish, poultry, omelets, lamb, stew, stuffing and tomato juice.

Mint   Aromatic with a cool flavor. Excellent in beverages, fish, lamb, cheese, soup, peas, carrots, and fruit desserts.

Oregano   Strong, aromatic odor. Use whole or ground in tomato juice, fish, eggs, pizza, omelets, chili, stew, gravy, poultry and vegetables.

Paprika   A bright red pepper, this spice is used in meat, vegetables and soups or as a garnish for potatoes, salads or eggs.

Parsley   Best when used fresh, but can be used dried as a garnish or as a seasoning. Try in fish, omelets, soup, meat, stuffing and mixed greens.

Rosemary   Very aromatic. Can be used fresh or dried. Season fish, stuffing, beef, lamb, poultry, onions, eggs, bread and potatoes. Great in dressings.

Saffron   Orange-yellow in color, this spice flavors or colors foods. Use in soup, chicken, rice and breads.

Sage   Use fresh or dried. The flowers are sometimes used in salads. May be used in tomato juice, fish, omelets, beef, poultry, stuffing, cheese spreads and breads.

Tarragon   Leaves have a pungent, hot taste. Use to flavor sauces, salads, fish, poultry, tomatoes, eggs, green beans, carrots and dressings.

Thyme   Sprinkle leaves on fish or poultry before broiling or baking. Throw a few sprigs directly on coals shortly before meat is finished grilling.

Baking Breads

Hints for Baking Breads

1. Kneading dough for 30 seconds after mixing improves the texture of baking powder biscuits.

2. Instead of shortening, use cooking or salad oil in waffles and hot cakes.

3. When bread is baking, a small dish of water in the oven will help keep the crust from hardening.

4. Dip a spoon in hot water to measure shortening, butter, etc., and the fat will slip out more easily.

5. Small amounts of leftover corn may be added to pancake batter for variety.

6. To make bread crumbs, use the fine cutter of a food grinder and tie a large paper bag over the spout in order to prevent flying crumbs.

7. When you are doing any sort of baking, you get better results if you remember to preheat your cookie sheet, muffin tins or cake pans.

Rules for Use of Leavening Agents

1. In simple flour mixtures, use 2 teaspoons baking powder to leaven 1 cup flour. Reduce this amount 1/2 teaspoon for each egg used.

2. To 1 teaspoon soda use 2 1/4 teaspoons cream of tartar, 2 cups freshly soured milk, or 1 cup molasses.

3. To substitute soda and an acid for baking powder, divide the amount of baking powder by 4. Take that as your measure and add acid according to rule 2.

Proportions of Baking Powder to Flour

biscuits	to 1 cup flour use 1 1/4 tsp. baking powder
cake with oil	to 1 cup flour use 1 tsp. baking powder
muffins	to 1 cup flour use 1 1/2 tsp. baking powder
popovers	to 1 cup flour use 1 1/4 tsp. baking powder
waffles	to 1 cup flour use 1 1/4 tsp. baking powder

Proportions of Liquid to Flour

drop batter	to 1 cup liquid use 2 to 2 1/2 cups flour
pour batter	to 1 cup liquid use 1 cup flour
soft dough	to 1 cup liquid use 3 to 3 1/2 cups flour
stiff dough	to 1 cup liquid use 4 cups flour

Time and Temperature Chart

Breads	Minutes	Temperature
biscuits	12 - 15	400° - 450°
cornbread	25 - 30	400° - 425°
gingerbread	40 - 50	350° - 370°
loaf	50 - 60	350° - 400°
nut bread	50 - 75	350°
popovers	30 - 40	425° - 450°
rolls	20 - 30	400° - 450°

Baking Desserts

Perfect Cookies

Cookie dough that is to be rolled is much easier to handle after it has been refrigerated for 10 to 30 minutes. This keeps the dough from sticking, even though it may be soft. If not done, the soft dough may require more flour and too much flour makes cookies hard and brittle. Place on a floured board only as much dough as can be easily managed. Flour the rolling pin slightly and roll lightly to desired thickness. Cut shapes close together and add trimmings to dough that needs to be rolled. Place pans or sheets in upper third of oven. Watch cookies carefully while baking in order to avoid burned edges. When sprinkling sugar on cookies, try putting it into a salt shaker in order to save time.

Perfect Pies

1. Pie crust will be better and easier to make if all the ingredients are cool.

2. The lower crust should be placed in the pan so that it covers the surface smoothly. Air pockets beneath the surface will push the crust out of shape while baking.

3. Folding the top crust over the lower crust before crimping will keep juices in the pie.

4. In making custard pie, bake at a high temperature for about ten minutes to prevent a soggy crust. Then finish baking at a low temperature.

5. When making cream pie, sprinkle crust with powdered sugar in order to prevent it from becoming soggy.

Perfect Cakes

1. Fill cake pans two-thirds full and spread batter into corners and sides, leaving a slight hollow in the center.

2. Cake is done when it shrinks from the sides of the pan or if it springs back when touched lightly with the finger.

3. After removing a cake from the oven, place it on a rack for about five minutes. Then, the sides should be loosened and the cake turned out on a rack in order to finish cooling.

4. Do not frost cakes until thoroughly cool.

5. Icing will remain where you put it if you sprinkle cake with powdered sugar first.

Time and Temperature Chart

Dessert	Time	Temperature
butter cake, layer	20-40 min.	380° - 400°
butter cake, loaf	40-60 min.	360° - 400°
cake, angel	50-60 min.	300° - 360°
cake, fruit	3-4 hrs.	275° - 325°
cake, sponge	40-60 min.	300° - 350°
cookies, molasses	18-20 min.	350° - 375°
cookies, thin	10-12 min.	380° - 390°
cream puffs	45-60 min.	300° - 350°
meringue	40-60 min.	250° - 300°
pie crust	20-40 min.	400° - 500°

Vegetables & Fruits

Vegetable	Cooking Method	Time
artichokes	boiled	40 min.
	steamed	45-60 min.
asparagus tips	boiled	10-15 min.
beans, lima	boiled	20-40 min.
	steamed	60 min.
beans, string	boiled	15-35 min.
	steamed	60 min.
beets, old	boiled or steamed	1-2 hours
beets, young with skin	boiled	30 min.
	steamed	60 min.
	baked	70-90 min.
broccoli, flowerets	boiled	5-10 min.
broccoli, stems	boiled	20-30 min.
brussels sprouts	boiled	20-30 min.
cabbage, chopped	boiled	10-20 min.
	steamed	25 min.
carrots, cut across	boiled	8-10 min.
	steamed	40 min.
cauliflower, flowerets	boiled	8-10 min.
cauliflower, stem down	boiled	20-30 min.
corn, green, tender	boiled	5-10 min.
	steamed	15 min.
	baked	20 min.
corn on the cob	boiled	8-10 min.
	steamed	15 min.
eggplant, whole	boiled	30 min.
	steamed	40 min.
	baked	45 min.
parsnips	boiled	25-40 min.
	steamed	60 min.
	baked	60-75 min.
peas, green	boiled or steamed	5-15 min.
potatoes	boiled	20-40 min.
	steamed	60 min.
	baked	45-60 min.
pumpkin or squash	boiled	20-40 min.
	steamed	45 min.
	baked	60 min.
tomatoes	boiled	5-15 min.
turnips	boiled	25-40 min.

Drying Time Table

Fruit	Sugar or Honey	Cooking Time
apricots	1/4 c. for each cup of fruit	about 40 min.
figs	1 T. for each cup of fruit	about 30 min.
peaches	1/4 c. for each cup of fruit	about 45 min.
prunes	2 T. for each cup of fruit	about 45 min.

Vegetables & Fruits

Buying Fresh Vegetables

Artichokes: Look for compact, tightly closed heads with green, clean-looking leaves. Avoid those with leaves that are brown or separated.

Asparagus: Stalks should be tender and firm; tips should be close and compact. Choose the stalks with very little white; they are more tender. Use asparagus soon because it toughens rapidly.

Beans, Snap: Those with small seeds inside the pods are best. Avoid beans with dry-looking pods.

Broccoli, Brussels Sprouts and Cauliflower: Flower clusters on broccoli and cauliflower should be tight and close together. Brussels sprouts should be firm and compact. Smudgy, dirty spots may indicate pests or disease.

Cabbage and Head Lettuce: Choose heads that are heavy for their size. Avoid cabbage with worm holes and lettuce with discoloration or soft rot.

Cucumbers: Choose long, slender cucumbers for best quality. May be dark or medium green, but yellow ones are undesirable.

Mushrooms: Caps should be closed around the stems. Avoid black or brown gills.

Peas and Lima Beans: Select pods that are well-filled but not bulging. Avoid dried, spotted, yellow, or flabby pods.

Buying Fresh Fruits

Bananas: Skin should be free of bruises and black or brown spots. Purchase them green and allow them to ripen at home at room temperature.

Berries: Select plump, solid berries with good color. Avoid stained containers which indicate wet or leaky berries. Berries with clinging caps, such as blackberries and raspberries, may be unripe. Strawberries without caps may be overripe.

Melons: In cantaloupes, thick, close netting on the rind indicates best quality. Cantaloupes are ripe when the stem scar is smooth and the space between the netting is yellow or yellow-green. They are best when fully ripe with fruity odor.

Honeydews are ripe when rind has creamy to yellowish color and velvety texture. Immature honeydews are whitish-green.

Ripe watermelons have some yellow color on one side. If melons are white or pale green on one side, they are not ripe.

Oranges, Grapefruit and Lemons: Choose those heavy for their size. Smoother, thinner skins usually indicate more juice. Most skin markings do not affect quality. Oranges with a slight greenish tinge may be just as ripe as fully colored ones. Light or greenish-yellow lemons are more tart than deep yellow ones. Avoid citrus fruits showing withered, sunken or soft areas.

Napkin Folding

General Tips:
Use well-starched linen napkins if possible. For more complicated folds, 24-inch napkins work best. Practice the folds with newspapers. Children can help. Once they learn the folds, they will have fun!

Shield

Easy fold. Elegant with monogram in corner.

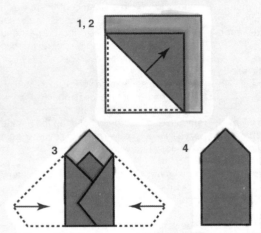

Instructions:
1. Fold into quarter size. If monogrammed, ornate corner should face down.
2. Turn up folded corner three-quarters.
3. Overlap right side and left side points.
4. Turn over; adjust sides so that they are even, single point in center.
5. Place point up or down on plate, or left of plate.

Rosette

Elegant on plate.

Instructions:
1. Fold left and right edges to center, leaving 1/2" opening along center.
2. Pleat firmly from top edge to bottom edge. Sharpen edges with hot iron.
3. Pinch center together. If necessary, use small piece of pipe cleaner to secure and top with single flower.
4. Spread out rosette.

Napkin Folding

Candle

Easy to do; can be decorated.

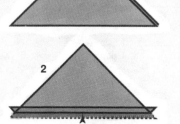

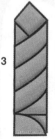

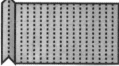

Instructions:
1. Fold into triangle, point at top.
2. Turn lower edge up 1".
3. Turn over, folded edge down.
4. Roll tightly from left to right.
5. Tuck in corner. Stand upright.

Fan

Pretty in napkin ring or on plate.

Instructions:
1. Fold top and bottom edges to center.
2. Fold top and bottom edges to center a second time.
3. Pleat firmly from the left edge. Sharpen edges with hot iron.
4. Spread out fan. Balance flat folds of each side on table. Well-starched napkins will hold shape.

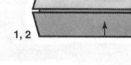

Lily

Effective and pretty on table.

Instructions:
1. Fold napkin into quarters.
2. Fold into triangle, closed corner to open points.
3. Turn two points over to other side. (Two points are on either side of closed point.)
4. Pleat.
5. Place closed end in glass. Pull down two points on each side and shape.

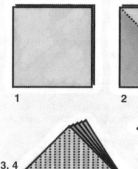

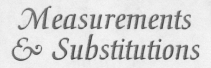

Measurements & Substitutions

Measurements

a pinch	⅛ teaspoon or less
3 teaspoons	1 tablespoon
4 tablespoons	¼ cup
8 tablespoons	½ cup
12 tablespoons	¾ cup
16 tablespoons	1 cup
2 cups	1 pint
4 cups	1 quart
4 quarts	1 gallon
8 quarts	1 peck
4 pecks	1 bushel
16 ounces	1 pound
32 ounces	1 quart
1 ounce liquid	2 tablespoons
8 ounces liquid	1 cup

**Use standard measuring spoons and cups.
All measurements are level.**

Substitutions

Ingredient	Quantity	Substitute
baking powder	1 teaspoon	¼ tsp. baking soda plus ½ tsp. cream of tartar
catsup or chili sauce	1 cup	1 c. tomato sauce plus ½ c. sugar and 2 T. vinegar (for use in cooking)
chocolate	1 square (1 oz.)	3 or 4 T. cocoa plus 1 T. butter
cornstarch	1 tablespoon	2 T. flour or 2 tsp. quick-cooking tapioca
cracker crumbs	¾ cup	1 c. bread crumbs
dates	1 lb.	1 ½ c. dates, pitted and cut
dry mustard	1 teaspoon	1 T. prepared mustard
flour, self-rising	1 cup	1 c. all-purpose flour, ½ tsp. salt, and 1 tsp. baking powder
herbs, fresh	1 tablespoon	1 tsp. dried herbs
milk, sour	1 cup	1 T. lemon juice or vinegar plus sweet milk to make 1 c. (let stand 5 minutes)
whole	1 cup	½ c. evaporated milk plus ½ c. water
min. marshmallows	10	1 lg. marshmallow
onion, fresh	1 small	1 T. instant minced onion, rehydrated
sugar, brown	½ cup	2 T. molasses in ½ c. granulated sugar
powdered	1 cup	1 c. granulated sugar plus 1 tsp. cornstarch
tomato juice	1 cup	½ c. tomato sauce plus ½ c. water

**When substituting cocoa for chocolate in cakes, the amount of flour must
be reduced. Brown and white sugars usually can be interchanged.**

Equivalency Chart

Food	Quantity	Yield
apple	1 medium	1 cup
banana, mashed	1 medium	1/3 cup
bread	1 1/2 slices	1 cup soft crumbs
bread	1 slice	1/4 cup fine, dry crumbs
butter	1 stick or 1/4 pound	1/2 cup
cheese, American, cubed	1 pound	2 2/3 cups
American, grated	1 pound	5 cups
cream cheese	3-ounce package	6 2/3 tablespoons
chocolate, bitter	1 square	1 ounce
cocoa	1 pound	4 cups
coconut	1 1/2 pound package	2 2/3 cups
coffee, ground	1 pound	5 cups
cornmeal	1 pound	3 cups
cornstarch	1 pound	3 cups
crackers, graham	14 squares	1 cup fine crumbs
saltine	28 crackers	1 cup fine crumbs
egg	4-5 whole	1 cup
whites	8-10	1 cup
yolks	10-12	1 cup
evaporated milk	1 cup	3 cups whipped
flour, cake, sifted	1 pound	4 1/2 cups
rye	1 pound	5 cups
white, sifted	1 pound	4 cups
white, unsifted	1 pound	3 3/4 cups
gelatin, flavored	3 1/4 ounces	1/2 cup
unflavored	1/4 ounce	1 tablespoon
lemon	1 medium	3 tablespoon juice
marshmallows	16	1/4 pound
noodles, cooked	8-ounce package	7 cups
uncooked	4 ounces (1 1/2 cups)	2-3 cups cooked
macaroni, cooked	8-ounce package	6 cups
macaroni, uncooked	4 ounces (1 1/4 cups)	2 1/4 cups cooked
spaghetti, uncooked	7 ounces	4 cups cooked
nuts, chopped	1/4 pound	1 cup
almonds	1 pound	3 1/2 cups
walnuts, broken	1 pound	3 cups
walnuts, unshelled	1 pound	1 1/2 to 1 3/4 cups
onion	1 medium	1/2 cup
orange	3-4 medium	1 cup juice
raisins	1 pound	3 1/2 cups
rice, brown	1 cup	4 cups cooked
converted	1 cup	3 1/2 cups cooked
regular	1 cup	3 cups cooked
wild	1 cup	4 cups cooked
sugar, brown	1 pound	2 1/2 cups
powdered	1 pound	3 1/2 cups
white	1 pound	2 cups
vanilla wafers	22	1 cup fine crumbs
zwieback, crumbled	4	1 cups

Food Quantities
For Large Servings

	25 Servings	50 Servings	100 Servings
Beverages:			
coffee	½ pound and 1 ½ gallons water	1 pound and 3 gallons water	2 pounds and 6 gallons water
lemonade	10-15 lemons and 1 ½ gallons water	20-30 lemons and 3 gallons water	40-60 lemons and 6 gallons water
tea	1/12 pound and 1 ½ gallons water	⅙ pound and 3 gallons water	⅓ pound and 6 gallons water
Desserts:			
layered cake	1 12" cake	3 10" cakes	6 10" cakes
sheet cake	1 10" x 12" cake	1 12" x 20" cake	2 12" x 20" cakes
watermelon	37 ½ pounds	75 pounds	150 pounds
whipping cream	¾ pint	1 ½ to 2 pints	3-4 pints
Ice cream:			
brick	3 ¼ quarts	6 ½ quarts	13 quarts
bulk	2 ¼ quarts	4 ½ quarts or 1 ¼ gallons	9 quarts or 2 ½ gallons
Meat, poultry or fish:			
fish	13 pounds	25 pounds	50 pounds
fish, fillets or steak	7 ½ pounds	15 pounds	30 pounds
hamburger	9 pounds	18 pounds	35 pounds
turkey or chicken	13 pounds	25 to 35 pounds	50 to 75 pounds
wieners (beef)	6 ½ pounds	13 pounds	25 pounds
Salads, casseroles:			
baked beans	¾ gallon	1 ¼ gallons	2 ½ gallons
jello salad	¾ gallon	1 ¼ gallons	2 ½ gallons
potato salad	4 ¼ quarts	2 ¼ gallons	4 ½ gallons
scalloped potatoes	4 ½ quarts or 1 12" x 20" pan	9 quarts or 2 ¼ gallons	18 quarts 4 ½ gallons
spaghetti	1 ¼ gallons	2 ½ gallons	5 gallons
Sandwiches:			
bread	50 slices or 3 1-pound loaves	100 slices or 6 1-pound loaves	200 slices or 12 1-pound loaves
butter	½ pound	1 pound	2 pounds
lettuce	1 ½ heads	3 heads	6 heads
mayonnaise	1 cup	2 cups	4 cups
mixed filling			
meat, eggs, fish	1 ½ quarts	3 quarts	6 quarts
jam, jelly	1 quart	2 quarts	4 quarts

Microwave Hints

1. Place an open box of hardened brown sugar in the microwave oven with 1 cup hot water. Microwave on high for 1 1/2 to 2 minutes for 1/2 pound or 2 to 3 minutes for 1 pound.

2. Soften hard ice cream by microwaving at 30% power. One pint will take 15 to 30 seconds; one quart, 30-45 seconds; and one-half gallon, 45-60 seconds.

3. To melt chocolate, place 1/2 pound in glass bowl or measuring cup. Melt uncovered at 50% power for 3-4 minutes; stir after 2 minutes.

4. Soften one 8-ounce package of cream cheese by microwaving at 30% power for 2 to 2 1/2 minutes. One 3-ounce package of cream cheese will soften in 1 1/2 to 2 minutes.

5. A 4 1/2 ounce carton of whipped topping will thaw in 1 minute on the defrost setting. Whipped topping should be slightly firm in the center, but it will blend well when stirred. Do not over thaw!

6. Soften jello that has set up too hard - perhaps you were to chill it until slightly thickened and forgot it. Heat on a low power setting for a very short time.

7. Heat hot packs. A wet fingertip towel will take about 25 seconds. It depends on the temperature of the water used to wet the towel.

8. To scald milk, cook 1 cup for 2 to 2 1/2 minutes, stirring once each minute.

9. To make dry bread crumbs, cut 6 slices of bread into 1/2-inch cubes. Microwave in 3-quart casserole 6-7 minutes, or until dry, stirring after 3 minutes. Crush in blender.

10. Refresh stale potato chips, crackers or other snacks of such type by putting a plateful in the microwave for 30-45 seconds. Let stand for 1 minute to crisp. Cereals can also be crisped.

11. Nuts will be easier to shell if you place 2 cups of nuts in a 1-quart casserole with 1 cup of water. Cook for 4 to 5 minutes and the nutmeats will slip out whole after cracking the shell.

12. Stamp collectors can place a few drops of water on a stamp to remove it from an envelope. Heat in the microwave for 20 seconds, and the stamp will come off.

13. Using a round dish instead of a square one eliminates overcooked corners in baking cakes.

14. Sprinkle a layer of medium, finely chopped walnuts evenly onto the bottom and side of a ring pan or bundt cake pan to enhances the looks and eating quality. Pour in batter and microwave as recipe directs.

15. Do not salt foods on the surface as it causes dehydration and toughens food. Salt after you remove from the oven unless the recipe calls for using salt in the mixture.

16. Heat left-over custard and use it as frosting for a cake.

17. Melt marshmallow cream. Half of a 7-ounce jar will melt in 35-40 seconds on high. Stir to blend.

18. To toast coconut, spread 1/2 cup coconut in a pie plate and cook for 3-4 minutes, stirring every 30 seconds after 2 minutes. Watch closely, as it quickly browns.

19. To melt crystallized honey, heat uncovered jar on high for 30-45 seconds. If jar is large, repeat.

20. One stick of butter or margarine will soften in 1 minute when microwaved at 20% power.

Calorie Counter

Beverages

apple juice, 6 oz. 90
coffee (black) 0
cola type, 12 oz. 115
cranberry juice, 6 oz. 115
ginger ale, 12 oz. 115
grape juice, (prepared from
    frozen concentrate), 6 oz. 142
lemonade, (prepared from
    frozen concentrate), 6 oz. 85
milk, protein fortified, 1 c. 105
    skim, 1 c. 90
    whole, 1 c. 160
orange juice, 6 oz. 85
pineapple juice, unsweetened, 6 oz. 95
root beer, 12 oz. 150
tonic (quinine water) 12 oz. 132

Breads

cornbread, 1 sm. square 130
dumplings, 1 med. 70
French toast, 1 slice 135
melba toast, 1 slice 25
muffins, blueberry, 1 muffin 110
    bran, 1 muffin.............................106
    corn, 1 muffin............................125
    English, 1 muffin 280
pancakes, 1 (4-in.) 60
pumpernickel, 1 slice 75
rye, 1 slice 60
waffle, 1 216
white, 1 slice 60-70
whole wheat, 1 slice 55-65

Cereals

cornflakes, 1 c. 105
cream of wheat, 1 c. 120
oatmeal, 1 c. 148
rice flakes, 1 c. 105
shredded wheat, 1 biscuit 100
sugar krisps, 3/4 c. 110

Crackers

graham, 1 cracker 15-30
rye crisp, 1 cracker..........................35
saltine, 1 cracker.........................17-20
wheat thins, 1 cracker 9

Dairy Products

butter or margarine, 1 T....................100
cheese, American, 1 oz. 100
    camembert, 1 oz. 85
    cheddar, 1 oz. 115
    cottage cheese, 1 oz. 30
    mozzarella, 1 oz. 90
    parmesan, 1 oz. 130
    ricotta, 1 oz. 50
    roquefort, 1 oz. 105
    Swiss, 1 oz. 105
cream, light, 1 T. 30
    heavy, 1 T. 55
    sour, 1 T. 45
hot chocolate, with milk, 1 c. 277
milk chocolate, 1 oz. 145-155
yogurt
    made w/ whole milk, 1 c. 150-165
    made w/ skimmed milk, 1 c. 125

Eggs

fried, 1 lg. 100
poached or boiled, 1 lg. 75-80
scrambled or in omelet, 1 lg. 110-130

Fish and Seafood

bass, 4 oz. 105
salmon, broiled or baked, 3 oz. 155
sardines, canned in oil, 3 oz. 170
trout, fried, 3 1/2 oz. 220
tuna, in oil, 3 oz. 170
    in water, 3 oz. 110

Calorie Counter

Fruits

apple, 1 med.	80-100
applesauce, sweetened, 1/2 c.	90-115
unsweetened, 1/2 c.	50
banana, 1 med.	85
blueberries, 1/2 c.	45
cantaloupe, 1/2 c.	24
cherries (pitted), raw, 1/2 c.	40
grapefruit, 1/2 med.	55
grapes, 1/2 c.	35-55
honeydew, 1/2 c.	55
mango, 1 med.	90
orange, 1 med.	65-75
peach, 1 med.	35
pear, 1 med.	60-100
pineapple, fresh, 1/2 c.	40
canned in syrup, 1/2 c.	95
plum, 1 med.	30
strawberries, fresh, 1/2 c.	30
frozen and sweetened, 1/2 c.	120-140
tangerine, 1 lg.	39
watermelon, 1/2 c.	42

Meat and Poultry

beef, ground (lean), 3 oz.	185
roast, 3 oz.	185
chicken, broiled, 3 oz.	115
lamb chop (lean), 3 oz.	175-200
steak, sirloin, 3 oz.	175
tenderloin, 3 oz.	174
top round, 3 oz.	162
turkey, dark meat, 3 oz.	175
white meat, 3 oz.	150
veal, cutlet, 3 oz.	156
roast, 3 oz.	76

Nuts

almonds, 2 T.	105
cashews, 2 T.	100
peanuts, 2 T.	105
peanut butter, 1 T.	95
pecans, 2 T.	95
pistachios, 2 T.	92
walnuts, 2 T.	80

Pasta

macaroni or spaghetti, cooked, 3/4 c.	115

Salad Dressings

blue cheese, 1 T.	70
French, 1 T.	65
Italian, 1 T.	80
mayonnaise, 1 T.	100
olive oil, 1 T.	124
Russian, 1 T.	70
salad oil, 1 T.	120

Soups

bean, 1 c.	130-180
beef noodle, 1 c.	70
bouillon and consomme, 1 c.	30
chicken noodle, 1 c.	65
chicken with rice, 1 c.	50
minestrone, 1 c.	80-150
split pea, 1 c.	145-170
tomato with milk, 1 c.	170
vegetable, 1 c.	80-100

Vegetables

asparagus, 1 c.	35
broccoli, cooked, 1/2 c.	25
cabbage, cooked, 1/2 c.	15-20
carrots, cooked, 1/2 c.	25-30
cauliflower, 1/2 c.	10-15
corn (kernels), 1/2 c.	70
green beans, 1 c.	30
lettuce, shredded, 1/2 c.	5
mushrooms, canned, 1/2 c.	20
onions, cooked, 1/2 c.	30
peas, cooked, 1/2 c.	60
potato, baked, 1 med.	90
chips, 8-10	100
mashed, w/milk & butter, 1 c.	200-300
spinach, 1 c.	40
tomato, raw, 1 med.	25
cooked, 1/2 c.	30

Cooking Terms

Au gratin: Topped with crumbs and/or cheese and browned in oven or under broiler.

Au jus: Served in its own juices.

Baste: To moisten foods during cooking with pan drippings or special sauce in order to add flavor and prevent drying.

Bisque: A thick cream soup.

Blanch: To immerse in rapidly boiling water and allow to cook slightly.

Cream: To soften a fat, especially butter, by beating it at room temperature. Butter and sugar are often creamed together, making a smooth, soft paste.

Crimp: To seal the edges of a two-crust pie either by pinching them at intervals with the fingers or by pressing them together with the tines of a fork.

Crudites: An assortment of raw vegetables (i.e. carrots, broccoli, celery, mushrooms) that is served as an hors d'oeuvre, often accompanied by a dip.

Degrease: To remove fat from the surface of stews, soups, or stock. Usually cooled in the refrigerator so that fat hardens and is easily removed.

Dredge: To coat lightly with flour, cornmeal, etc.

Entree: The main course.

Fold: To incorporate a delicate substance, such as whipped cream or beaten egg whites, into another substance without releasing air bubbles. A spatula is used to gently bring part of the mixture from the bottom of the bowl to the top. The process is repeated, while slowly rotating the bowl, until the ingredients are thoroughly blended.

Glaze: To cover with a glossy coating, such as a melted and somewhat diluted jelly for fruit desserts.

Julienne: To cut vegetables, fruits, or cheeses into match-shaped slivers.

Marinate: To allow food to stand in a liquid in order to tenderize or to add flavor.

Meuniére: Dredged with flour and sautéed in butter.

Mince: To chop food into very small pieces.

Parboil: To boil until partially cooked; to blanch. Usually final cooking in a seasoned sauce follows this procedure.

Pare: To remove the outermost skin of a fruit or vegetable.

Poach: To cook gently in hot liquid kept just below the boiling point.

Purée: To mash foods by hand by rubbing through a sieve or food mill, or by whirling in a blender or food processor until perfectly smooth.

Refresh: To run cold water over food that has been parboiled in order to stop the cooking process quickly.

Sauté: To cook and/or brown food in a small quantity of hot shortening.

Scald: To heat to just below the boiling point, when tiny bubbles appear at the edge of the saucepan.

Simmer: To cook in liquid just below the boiling point. The surface of the liquid should be barely moving, broken from time to time by slowly rising bubbles.

Steep: To let food stand in hot liquid in order to extract or to enhance flavor, like tea in hot water or poached fruit in sugar syrup.

Toss: To combine ingredients with a repeated lifting motion.

Whip: To beat rapidly in order to incorporate air and produce expansion, as in heavy cream or egg whites.